IS DIVORCE A SIN?

Four Choices for
Troubled Marriages

By
Garry D. Zeigler

FAITH ONE
PUBLISHING

LOS ANGELES, CALIFORNIA

Unless otherwise indicated, all Scripture quotations are taken from either the *King James Version* or the *New King James Version* of the Bible. Copyright 1979, 1980, 1982 by Thomas Nelson, Inc. Publishers. Used by permission. Printed in the United States of America.

IS DIVORCE A SIN?
Four Choices for Troubled Marriages
ISBN 1-883798-37-X
Copyright 1999 by
Faith One Publishing
P.O. Box 90000
Los Angeles, CA 90009

Published by Faith One Publishing
7901 South Vermont Avenue
Los Angeles, CA 90044

Printed in the United States of America

Publisher's Cataloging-in-Publication
(Provided by Quality Books, Inc.)

Zeigler, Garry D.
    Is divorce a sin? : four choices for troubled
    marriages / by Garry D. Zeigler — 1st ed.
        p. cm.
        ISBN: 1-883798-37-X

        1. Divorce—Religious aspects—Christianity.
    2. Domestic relations.   I. Title.

    BT707.Z45 1999   248.8'44
                                      QBI99-1245

DEDICATION

I want to express my sincere gratitude to Pastor Frederick K.C. Price for his instruction, guidance, and influence in my life, which have enabled me to produce this work. I thank God for his commitment to Christ and for the example of integrity that he has set for me to follow.

To my wife Antonia and our four beautiful children — Sylvia, Antonia, Garry II, and Lloren — who have patiently supported me during the preparation of this work: I love you, appreciate you, and thank God for your being a part of my life.

I also would like to acknowledge Mrs. Angela M. Evans and Mrs. Cheryl A. Crabbe for their commitment to seeing this book come to fruition. Their confidence in this work is truly a blessing. I am also very grateful to Bobby L. Kennedy for the generous use of his resources and Pastor L. Craig Hays for his encouragement, patience, and understanding throughout the writing of this book.

My sincere appreciation also goes to the unnamed host of others whose contributions and efforts, whether large or small, have aided in the realization of this work. May God richly bless them all.

And finally, thanks be to God, who allows our light to shine so that others may see our good works and glorify Him. He truly is a good God.

TABLE OF CONTENTS

FOREWORD

I know of very few books dealing with the issue of divorce that are as bold and as captivating as Garry D. Zeigler's *Is Divorce a Sin?* This hard-hitting, thought-provoking teaching by Pastor Garry, one of the assistant pastors on my staff at Crenshaw Christian Center, is bound to set many people free from the guilt, entanglements, confusion and pressures that accompany troubled marriages.

Is Divorce a Sin? overflows with revelation, and it will undoubtedly overturn previous notions about divorce and separation. Garry makes us understand that the same God who instituted marriage also instituted divorce, because of the hardness of men's hearts.

And men's hearts are apparently getting harder. According to a recent poll conducted by the Barna Research Organization, each year nearly half of all the marriages in the United States end in divorce. This is a shocking statistic, but it is even more alarming when you consider that approximately 27 percent of born-again Christians have been divorced, while only 23 percent of non-Christians have been divorced.

If you are trapped in a troubled marriage and considering the options of divorce or separation, *Is Divorce a Sin?* is timely reading that will help you make an informed decision. I highly

IS DIVORCE A SIN?

recommend this insightful teaching for those suffering through troubled marriages and for their counselors.

> *— Frederick K.C. Price*
> *Pastor*
> *Crenshaw Christian Center*
> *Home of the FaithDome*
> *Los Angeles, California*

PREFACE

During the first years of my marriage to Garry Zeigler I discovered I had a lot of selfishness to overcome if our marriage was going to be a success. I had been raised in a single-parent home, was an only child, and was accustomed to constantly having my own way. Marriage does not work like this; there is a tremendous amount of compromising both parties must be willing to do if their marriage is to be the blessing that God intends it to be. Learning to compromise was a particularly huge hurdle for me, but it was necessary so that Garry and I could be on one accord and make our marriage last.

I also had to learn how to communicate with my husband. I was not used to sitting down to settle an issue. Thank God Garry had come from a large two-parent home; he understood the importance of communication, so he insisted we talk about everything. Although this was hard for me at first, it has turned out to be such a blessing. For example, when Garry learned that I did not particularly like cleaning the kitchen, he offered to take care of this responsibility and has been doing so ever since. Consequently, as I have learned more and more about my husband, I have taken responsibility for doing certain things that I know will make his life easier. Garry and I have resolved every challenge in our marriage to our mutual benefit by taking the time to talk and to look to the Bible as our final authority to resolve the issue. There is no doubt in my mind that because of Garry's communication skills and our use of God's Word as our guide, our marriage survived.

My hope is that as you are reading what Garry has to share, you will start to see how you, too, can overcome any tough times you may be having in your marriage. But while most of what Garry has to say focuses on what you can do about a spouse whose lifestyle is contrary to what God says in His Word, you still need to keep in mind the part you have played in bringing your marriage to where it is now. Consider yourself. The Bible says if you first judge yourself, you will not be judged (1 Corinthians 11:31). You may discover, as I did, that there is something that you need to do — or that *you could do* — that would help turn your marriage around. You may find there are things you personally must overcome if you want your marriage to last. At first these challenges may seem insurmountable, but I can tell you from experience that God will be there every step of the way to see you through if you put your trust in Him.

I also urge you to seek the Lord as to how you should apply what you are about to learn to your own marriage and family. Only the Father God, by His Word found in the Bible and by His Spirit, can give you the guidance and direction that is best for you. When you know in your heart what you need to do, that is the leading of the Lord — just do it. It may not always make sense, but as long as you can see in the Bible what you already know in your heart, then you are on the right track. This is when your "doing it" becomes faith. God will honor your faith as long as you continue to seek Him step by step.

After almost 20 years and four children, I can say without hesitation that Garry and I are very happily married. Because of our commitment to doing what is right before the Lord and our willingness to work together to become one, our marriage is like a well-polished diamond. Garry and I have become the best of friends. I truly love him, and I thank God for such a wonderful husband and a beautiful family.

— *Antonia Zeigler*

INTRODUCTION

What I am about to share with you is some of the wisdom the Lord has given me in His Word for overcoming a troubled marriage. But do not take my word for it – do not just act on what I am telling you. Take the time to open your Bible and see for yourself what the Lord is saying about your marriage. Use the information I am about to share with you as a foundation for seeking what the Lord would have you do to turn the stumbling blocks in your marriage into steppingstones. I guarantee you that if you trust in the Lord and act on His Word, you will come out on top.

You may ask: "But how do I know this trouble in my marriage is not meant to be?" John 10:10 quotes Jesus, who is the Living Word, as saying:

"The thief does not come except to steal, and to kill, and to destroy. I have come that they may have life, and that they may have it more abundantly."

Jesus came to give you an abundant life. Having challenges in your marital relationship hardly constitutes an abundant life. After all, it was the heavenly Father who ordained marriage and said it is not good for man to be alone (Genesis 2:15), so He certainly must want you to prosper in your marital relationship.

"Yes, but I have learned so much by what I have gone through," you say. Well, tell me why God would want you to go through confusion, pain, and heartache when He loves you? It is great that you have matured, but learning by experience is not the only way to learn. For example, after you burn out the engine in your car, you learn that you should have changed your oil every 3,000 miles. But wouldn't it have been far better if you had just read the manufacturer's instructions for maintenance? That way, you could have avoided damaging your car. Well, the Bible is your original owner's manual.

This book is designed to give you godly options to apply to your troubled marriage so you can make the changes necessary to have peace in your family. I applaud you for having enough concern about your marriage that you would take the time to seek godly wisdom. Now just be sure that you apply what you are learning. Remember, faith requires action — acting on what God's Word directs you to do.

Since I use the New King James Version of the Bible in my daily counseling as a pastor, I will also use this same translation throughout this book (unless otherwise stated). I trust this teaching will be a blessing to you, as it is intended to give you greater insight into the very heart and character of our loving heavenly Father who created and designed marriage and the family to be the ultimate blessing in our lives.

ONE

MAKING PLANS FOR GODLY CHANGE

During the time of the prophet Isaiah, the nation of Israel was surrounded by smaller polytheistic nations that were involved in all sorts of idolatry. These nations had entwined Israel in their finances, general commerce, and all kinds of political entanglements. The children of Israel knew that these relationships were ungodly and that these smaller nations did not have Israel's best interests at heart. But their financial and political interdependence made them unwilling to make a change. It was not until they realized that they were no longer being blessed financially and no longer sleeping securely that they were willing to let God show them a better way.

The children of Israel knew that their God was the only living God. They remembered how He had delivered them from Egypt, parted the Red Sea for their forefathers while drowning pharaoh's army in its depths, and given them manna from heaven. The children of Israel left Egypt with great wealth. Their elderly were not feeble, and their sick were instantly made well. Their clothes and shoes did not wear out while they wandered in the desert. But now they were no longer enjoying the supernatural manifestations of God's favor. They recognized that they were not being kept in the style to which they had become accustomed, so they knew something was wrong.

That was when the Lord began to talk to Israel through the Prophet Isaiah. The Lord first let Israel know that they were going to have to make some changes. But when they began to consider making a change, they wondered how they could overcome the realities that such a change would bring. God answered them from Isaiah 54:2-3:

> "Enlarge the place of your tent, and let them stretch out the curtains of your dwellings; do not spare; lengthen your cords, and strengthen your stakes.
>
> For you shall expand to the right and to the left, and your descendants will inherit the nations, and make the desolate cities inhabited."

God assured the nation of Israel that they would be blessed once they conformed to His way and prepared themselves to receive His blessings. He gave them His Word that their lives would be better if they trusted in Him. In fact, their lives would be so much better that they would need to pull up their tent stakes and lengthen its cords. The Lord God told them to make plans for increase, not decrease.

Likewise, the Spirit of God is calling those whose marital relationship is ungodly, in the sense that it is not bringing the fulfillment, joy, and peace that God intends marriage to be, to make a godly change. He says to prepare for the blessings that go with change, not for the negative consequences that you fear such a change will bring.

Who is Going to Pay the Bills?

Like Israel, another concern a spouse may have regarding making a change is "Can I expect to make it on my own financially?" Israel wanted to know if they were going to be blessed financially if they made a change. God answered their concern in Isaiah 54:11-12:

"O you afflicted one, tossed with tempest, and not comforted, behold, I will lay your stones with colorful gems, and lay your foundations with sapphires.

I will make your pinnacles of rubies, your gates of crystal, and all your walls of precious stones."

Sounds like God's answer is a resounding yes! He promised Israel that He would take care of them financially, if they decided to make a change for the purpose of reaching His best. God told Israel, which represents a type of spouse in a troubled marriage, that He was going to be the one who supplied their needs. The same is true of you. If you trust God, make a change for the sake of having God's best in your life, and then allow Him to be your Provider, He will show you how to walk in abundance despite the circumstances. He will show you how to prosper through your change.

Not only does God promise to take care of Israel, the troubled spouse, but He commits Himself to taking care of

3

them in grand fashion. God says they would set their feet upon steppingstones of valuable jewels. They would see their borders were made with precious stones. He would take care of them so well that they would have walls inlaid with jewels. Nothing would be lacking.

God is also letting you know that He is not going to come up short in taking care of those who see Him as their Provider. The Apostle Paul knew this to be true. Paul came from a wealthy family and was accustomed to the very best life had to offer; Paul knew what it meant to be taken care of. This is why when Paul told the Philippians that **My God shall supply all your need according to His riches in glory by Christ Jesus** (Philippians 4:19), it really encouraged the Church at Philippi. They knew that Paul knew what he was talking about.

The heavenly Father wants you to not limit Him. He wants you to know that He is the Lord your God, who will provide for you at all times. In fact, He is Jehovah-jireh, which translated means "The LORD will provide," just as Abraham said in Genesis 22:14:

> **And Abraham called the name of the place, The-LORD-Will-Provide; as it is said to this day, "In the Mount of the LORD it shall be provided."**

And just as God provided the ram in the thicket to replace Abraham's only son as the sacrifice, the heavenly Father is willing and able to provide for you. In fact, Ephesians 3:20 says He is **...able to do exceedingly abundantly above all that we ask or think, according to the power that works in us....**

4

Once you make God your Provider, you will begin to see that you do not have to put up with your spouse's ungodly behavior. You can make a change, and this change will not be for shrinkage, but for expansion and betterment. You have God's Word on it.

Who Will My Children Look Up To?

The next question usually asked is "Who will be a role model for my children? I want them to have someone to look up to, and at least my spouse has been a kind of a leader in the home. So if my spouse leaves, this will affect our children."

Israel asked similar questions regarding their posterity. They realized their children needed a positive influence and instruction in a solid way of living. What would be the outcome for their children if they considered a change? God assured Israel by committing Himself to instructing their children. In Isaiah 54:13, the Spirit of God says,

All your children shall be taught by the LORD,
and great shall be the peace of your children.

Isn't it wonderful to know the Lord is willing to be the leader in your home? God puts Himself on the line; He says He will teach your children Himself. God does not lack intelligence and He knows how to teach, so you know your children will learn. Jesus said in John 14:26 that:

"The Holy Spirit, whom the Father will send in
My name, He will teach you all things and bring to
your remembrance all things that I said to you."

5

The Holy Spirit is the Teacher, and He instructs you from the Word of God. First Corinthians 2:13 says:

These things we also speak, not in words which man's wisdom teaches but which the Holy Spirit teaches, comparing spiritual things with spiritual.

One of the ways the Holy Spirit teaches is by comparing spiritual things with spiritual; He teaches by comparison or example. You see this in the New Testament with Jesus, who is often quoted in the Gospels as teaching in parables. Parables are short stories or analogies that illustrate a principle or a truth. Because these parables use things that are common or familiar to convey what needs to be learned, a student is able to get a clearer picture of the information being conveyed. The student learns by example — and the Holy Spirit knows exactly what examples will work best for your children. He knows your children, so He knows how to get and keep their attention. This is why He is called *the* Teacher — not just *a* teacher.

The heavenly Father wants to start teaching your children by showing them the right way rather than the wrong way they are learning from their disobedient parent who is acting contrary to what God says in the Bible. If you will trust that God is all that He says He is and make the changes He tells you are necessary, your children will no longer experience the frustration, anger, resentment, and disappointment that comes from seeing mommy and daddy fighting. God says **Great shall be the peace of your children.** He will bring peace upon your children, a peace you have not seen in them because of your challenged relationship.

Of course, you should be concerned about losing the male or female role model in the lives of your children. But, with an ungodly-acting mate, aren't you providing an environment for your children that is hazardous and void of peace just to keep what you believe is some sense of leadership in your home? Besides that, if a woman or a man is not acting like a godly wife or husband, then what kind of role model are they really? You need to know that God says He is prepared to step in and be all that you need.

Who Will Protect My Home?

"How am I going to protect my children and me? After all, you see all kinds of news reports of people and families getting hurt and murdered. At least I know what to expect when my spouse comes in the door, stumbling out of a stupor of drugs, alcohol, or whatever." This is a hard decision to make. Spouses in challenged marital relationships often, out of fear, convince themselves to accept their status because they don't want to give anyone else the opportunity of being destructive in their lives. So, they will opt to deal with a bad spouse who they at least are familiar with.

If you are wondering who is going to protect you and your children, take a look at what the Bible says in Isaiah 54:15-16:

> **Indeed they shall surely assemble, but not because of Me. Whoever assembles against you shall fall for your sake.**
>
> **Behold, I have created the blacksmith who blows the coals in the fire, who brings forth an**

**instrument for his work; and I have created the
spoiler to destroy.**

God is saying He will take care of you and your family
physically — and woe be to the person who would come
against you when God is protecting you. In Isaiah 54:17,
God promises:

**No weapon formed against you shall prosper
and every tongue which rises against you in judg-
ment you shall condemn. This is the heritage of
the servants of the LORD, and their righteousness is from Me," says the LORD.**

You do not have to worry about living in an evil and
perverse world, because God says He is going to take care
of you, if you trust Him.

Isaiah 54 tells you that a godly change, a change that is
based upon what God says in His Word, is positive — that
it is for blessings and expansion. The Scripture guarantees
that God will take care of you financially and make provisions for you, whereas before you may not have seen how
you would survive. It also lets you know that the Lord will
take care of your children and teach them Himself. And finally, the Lord says He will provide physical protection for
you and your household. Obviously, the Father is serious
about wanting His children to make the godly changes necessary to enjoy the abundant life in Christ Jesus.

So, if you are having challenges with your marriage
and are just waiting for God to turn it all around for you,
then you are in for a disappointment. This passage from the
Book of Isaiah lets you know that you are going to have to

make some changes in your marital relationship based upon the promises God has given you in His Word. The Lord has already done all He is going to do in your relationship by giving you everything you need in the wisdom and promises of His Word. All you have to do is to find out what the Bible has to say about your need and then do what God says in it. That is faith — acting on what God's Word tells you to do.

So the question is not "Why won't God?" but rather "Why won't you?" There will not be any positive changes in your marital relationship until you take action based upon godly wisdom. You are going to have to go beyond the circumstances that are challenging your marriage by doing what God's Word tells you to do. And you can — if you put your trust in Him.

This, of course, won't be easy. In fact, the Apostle Paul called it a *press* in Philippians 3:14:

I press toward the goal for the prize of the upward call of God in Christ Jesus.

In other words, reaching the prize of the upward call of God in Christ Jesus — obtaining God's best in your marital relationship — is going to take some effort. It will undoubtedly be a *press*. But until you press through and determine that you are not going to allow your present circumstances or the way you feel to deter you from having the abundant life in Christ Jesus, your marriage is not likely to change for the better. You are going to have to set aside everything that would stand between you and what God says that your marriage should be.

In Psalm 78, we see how detrimental it can be to allow your circumstances and the way you think and feel to come between you and what the Lord has for you. In this Psalm, the Bible says the children of Israel limited the Holy One by refusing to believe His Word and make a change. They refused to go into the Promised Land and take what God said was theirs. Verses 40 through 42 say that the children of Israel did not remember His power; they forgot how He redeemed them from their enemy:

> **How often they provoked Him in the wilderness, and grieved Him in the desert!**
> **Yes, again and again they tempted God, and limited the Holy One of Israel.**
> **They did not remember His power: the day when He redeemed them from the enemy.**

The children of Israel were afraid to possess the land; they were afraid to believe what God had told them. Fear caused them to limit God's power in their lives. They stopped themselves from receiving all that God had for them. Don't let this happen to you. Fear should have no place in you. Second Timothy 1:7 says:

> **For God has not given us a spirit of fear, but of power and of love and of a sound mind.**

So you see, as a person committed to living a godly life, you have no business entertaining fear because it is not of God. It is by confessing what the Word of God says over any fearful situation that you eliminate this bondage in your life.

When you think about it, there never is need to fear. You have the assurance of knowing that the Lord will never leave you nor forsake you (Hebrews 13:5), that no weapon formed against you shall prosper (Isaiah 54:17), and that the angel of the Lord encamps around and about you (Psalm 34:7). You also know that you can expect to make wise decisions because you have the Word of God and the Holy Spirit as your unfailing guide.

Less Than God's Best

If your spouse does not want the marital relationship to grow and prosper, you have the option of letting everything continue as it is. But, then you must be willing to live with the reality that your marriage relationship will never be fulfilled. You must be willing to settle for less than God's best. The decision is yours.

One definition of insanity is to do what you have always done and yet keep expecting a different result. If you say your desire is to just maintain what you have in your marriage relationship, but secretly you are hoping your spouse will change for the better, you are setting yourself up for great disappointment. Ask yourself these questions: "Can I really keep everything the same and maintain my sanity?" "Can I be satisfied with being permanently unhappy?" "Am I willing to accept less than God's best?" God has given you a free will, so the decision is up to you. He is not going to make you or your spouse do anything, nor is He going to make decisions for you. You have to step out in faith and then He will be there every step of the way to help and guide you.

TWO

THE FIRST CHOICE: TOLERATION

An abused wife says, "Pastor, my husband is beating me and refuses to change his ways, but I am committed to staying with him." A discouraged husband comments, "I hope my wife isn't drunk when I get home tonight."

Both husbands and wives have admitted to me that they avoid going home because they do not want to deal with their spouse's foul mouth, denigration, and fits of anger.

Despite such dissatisfactions, many couples choose to allow things to remain the same within their marriages. They continue unfulfilled at best. They do not realize that it takes more energy to *tolerate* a dysfunctional marriage than it does to initiate the changes necessary to have a wonderful and fulfilling relationship.

If you are in a troubled marriage and you and your spouse have the attitude that you are going to just keep everything the same, then you need to understand this basic principle:

If you always do what you have always done,
you will always get what you have always got!

So, the first option is to let things remain the same, and to simply put up with things as they are. While this certainly is not the way to resolve a marital problem, it nonetheless is an option. With neither you nor your spouse willing to do anything to bring about a positive change, your marital relationship will remain tolerable at best. You need to know that there are godly changes you can make that will cause your marriage to prosper, and that God will see you through these changes as long as they are executed with the wisdom that comes from Him alone.

After all, when all is said and done, will it really have been worth it not to change? Is it worth it to spend the next 30 or 40 years married to a drug addict, a whoremonger, or a spouse-abuser? How long are you willing to wait? How much abuse are you willing to take? How much are you worth? How important is it for your children to have a sense of stability and peace in your home?

You may be thinking, "I vowed I would stay with him or her through richer and poorer, through good times and bad, through sickness and in health, and until death do us part." Well, there is a difference between sticking with some-one through the unintentional and unforeseen ill circum-stances and staying with someone who deliberately chooses to do wrong.

God never intended that you be your spouse's savior. If you have done all that you know to do to help your spouse do what is best for him or her and your family, then you are no longer responsible for your spouse's actions. If your spouse is not willing to change his or her destructive and abusive habits, then do not allow yourself to be sucked into the trap of feeling responsible for their decisions. Do not start thinking that you can somehow change your partner. God has given every man and woman a free will. The heavenly Father will not violate any person's free will, nor will He give you the power to do so. The Lord only holds you accountable for yourself and what has been entrusted to your care.

In John 10:10, Jesus says He came so you might have life more abundantly. This is God's desire for you; this is why He sent His Son. Don't let what Jesus did for you be in vain by staying with someone who does not treat you right.

If your spouse does not want your marital relationship to grow and prosper, you have the option of letting everything remain the same. But, then you must be willing to accept and live with that prospect. You must realize you have made the decision to settle for less than God's best. But if you have children, you need to take into consideration what your negative relationship with your spouse is doing to them. Is this the example you want to set for them to follow?

THREE

THE SECOND CHOICE: SEPARATION

You may be thinking, "Okay, say I want to make a change in my marital relationship in order to have God's best; what other options should I consider?" A second option is separation. But let me make this clear from the start: Separation is not God's desire for a married couple. God desires that families stay together, be one flesh, and live in marital bliss by enjoying the blessings that come with His divine order for true and happy matrimony.

Regardless of the circumstances surrounding your marriage, God intended that your vows be sacred. He meant for your marriage covenant to be as significant to the both of you as it is to Him. After all, He ordained marriage (Genesis 2:24). The Bible says in Genesis 2:18 that after the Lord put man in the garden of Eden to tend and keep it, He said:

"It is not good that man should be alone; I will make him a helper comparable to him."

17

IS DIVORCE A SIN?

Evidently, you need your marriage partner, so when you are separated you cannot enjoy God's best.

Separation is the suspension of cohabitation either by mutual consent or by order of a court. It means that you are no longer dwelling together as a couple and enjoying normal relations. Your spouse may decide, "I'm going to stay in this house, while you go to a hotel." Or, one of you may return home to live with parents or just move to a different location altogether. In any of these or other possible living arrangements, the bottom line is that you and your spouse are living apart as a result of the severity of the conditions within your marriage.

Separation provides a means whereby both parties can come to the realization that they need each other and are better off together than apart. It is supposed to get the attention of the spouse who is in the wrong, letting him or her know that if changes are not made then something is going to be lost. Separation, however, was never intended to be a precondition for divorce.

Separation also gets the attention of others who care about you and your spouse. You cannot hide indefinitely from parents, in-laws, children, relatives, friends, or your pastor. The people who love you will eventually want to know what happened and what if anything they can do to help. Separation gives them — people who normally would not get involved — the opportunity to help resolve the issues challenging your happiness. The pain of separation can then have the positive result of bringing everyone closer together.

Because separation is supposed to arrest the attention of the spouse who is delinquent in the marital covenant, there must be an understanding that there will not be sexual relations. In this way, the separation can be an effective means for drawing each spouse's attention toward quickly resolving the marital challenges. If you are separated from your spouse but still having intimate relations, you are defeating the purpose. Resolving the challenges will not be as advantageous or needful to the partner who is in the wrong if sexual pleasure is still being enjoyed.

Purpose and Principles of Marriage

The purpose of marriage is intimate, physical fulfillment. This is evident in the principles the Apostle Paul gave to the Church of Corinth. In 1 Corinthians 7:1-16, Paul wrote:

Now concerning the things of which you wrote to me: It is good for a man not to touch a woman.

Nevertheless, because of sexual immorality, let each man have his own wife, and let each woman have her own husband.

Let the husband render to his wife the affection due her, and likewise also the wife to her husband.

The wife does not have authority over her own body, but the husband does. And likewise the husband does not have authority over his own body, but the wife does.

Do not deprive one another except with consent for a time, that you may give yourselves to fasting and prayer; and come together again so that Satan does not tempt you because of your lack of self-control.

But I say this as a concession, not as a commandment.

For I wish that all men were even as I myself. But each one has his own gift from God, one in this manner and another in that.

But I say to the unmarried and to the widows: It is good for them if they remain even as I am;

But if they cannot exercise self-control, let them marry. For it is better to marry than to burn with passion.

Now to the married I command, yet not I but the Lord: A wife is not to depart from her husband.

But even if she does depart, let her remain unmarried or be reconciled to her husband. And a husband is not to divorce his wife.

But to the rest I, not the Lord, say: If any brother has a wife who does not believe, and she is willing to live with him, let him not divorce her.

And a woman who has a husband who does not believe, if he is willing to live with her, let her not divorce him.

For the unbelieving husband is sanctified by the wife, and the unbelieving wife is sanctified by the husband; otherwise your children would be unclean, but now they are holy.

But if the unbeliever departs, let him depart; a brother or a sister is not under bondage in such cases. But God has called us to peace.

For how do you know, O wife, whether you will save your husband? Or how do you know, O husband, whether you will save your wife?

Paul addresses the principles of marriage by stating it is better to remain single. But, he immediately goes on to say, **Nevertheless, because of sexual immorality, let each man have his own wife, and let each woman have her own husband.** Paul then says that the purpose of marriage is intimate, physical fulfillment. This is why Paul adds later that within the marriage covenant **Let the husband render to his wife the affection due her, and likewise also the wife to her husband.**

The word *due*, within the context of this verse, means "that which is owed." The original King James Version translates the word *affection* as "benevolence." *Benevolence* means "a good behavior." Showing good behavior or affection toward your spouse includes fulfilling your commitment to intimate, physical relations. Through the writings of the Apostle Paul, the Spirit of God is saying that if you are going to marry, then you are to be prepared to fulfill your physical, intimate commitment toward your spouse.

It is important that, as a married couple, you recognize that when you agreed to marry, you said you would be responsible to each other physically. Your spouse became responsible for meeting this need in your life and you became responsible for meeting your spouse's need.

Hebrews 13:4 is a witness to 1 Corinthians 7:1-16. This Scripture says:

> **Marriage is honorable among all, and the bed undefiled; but fornicators and adulterers God will judge.**

This Scripture tells you that marriage, as a means of fulfilling the God-given need for intimate physical expres-

21

sion, is honorable and therefore right in the eyes of God. Consequently, God will judge others because there is no excuse for going outside the marital relationship for physical intimacy. God intended that you would have your satisfaction in each other, and He would bless it.

When I made a commitment to marry my wife, I determined I was no longer going to live as a single man. I committed to being with my wife, and no other, in a physically intimate way. I agreed that my body would belong to her and her body would belong to me. I knew marriage was for me because when I was single I had no godly way of satisfying my physical urges in an intimate capacity without sinning. So if you are single, be holy and celibate. But once you get married, realize you have made a commitment to be holy and sexually fulfilled in your spouse.

If you do not have sex with your spouse, you are in sin. If you violate this marital responsibility, you leave both you and your spouse open to enticement by Satan. The Bible says Satan will come in with temptations. This is why the Bible clearly indicates that intimate, physical relations are a marital responsibility.

Proverbs 5:15-20 paints a picture of a godly intimate relationship:

> **Drink water from your own cistern, and running water from your own well.**
> **Should your fountains be dispersed abroad, streams of water in the streets?**
> **Let them be only your own, and not for strangers with you.**

Let your fountain be blessed, and rejoice with the wife of your youth.

As a loving deer and a graceful doe, let her breasts satisfy you at all times; and always be enraptured with her love.

For why should you, my son, be enraptured by an immoral woman, And be embraced in the arms of a seductress?

This Scripture compares a well of running water to the wife's contribution to the marriage. The same is true of the husband's contribution. You are leaving your spouse open to frustration and even anger when you deny your mate your body. Did you notice that the well is described as *running* water? This implies that the water supply is in abundance, is a constant and powerful force. So, too, should your physical, intimate relations be in your marriage. Consequently, this area of marital responsibility is not to be toyed with.

This is why the Bible says in 1 Corinthians 7:4:

The wife does not have authority over her own body, but the husband does. And likewise the husband does not have authority over his own body, but the wife does.

Now, some husbands have said, "Well, honey, your body belongs to me. I want you, and that's just the way it is, regardless of how you feel." Then, when they get angry and upset with their wives, they say, "Well, I'm not going to do anything tonight." This is wrong because the man's body does not belong to him; it belongs to his wife. If his wife says she desires his body, then he must fulfill his responsi-

23

bility as a spouse. He cannot say, "I'm the man of this house. I'm the head of this home, and I decide when we are going to have intimacy because that is my right." He has no such right. Both spouses are supposed to see physical intimacy as a responsibility they have to one another.

First Corinthians 7:5 goes on to make this very clear. This verse explains:

> **Do not deprive one another except with consent for a time, that you may give yourselves to fasting and prayer; and come together again so that Satan does not tempt you because of your lack of self-control.**

This sounds like God knows His people; He knows what they need. So He has made provision for their needs in His Word. *Consent* means there is a mutual agreement. Biblically speaking, it is wrong to tell your spouse you are not going to honor your marriage covenant when you are able, unless you have mutually agreed that you will fast and pray for a period. This, of course, excludes times of mental and physical illness, as well as pregnancy. Otherwise, if without prior consent, you or your spouse say you want to fast and pray and therefore will not be able to fulfill your responsibilities as a spouse, you are wrong. If you or your spouse have done this, the Bible refers to it as depriving or, as the King James translation says, "defrauding" one another.

I believe the word *defraud* is a more accurate depiction of what the Scripture is teaching marriage partners. *Defraud* means that you have married with the intent of not meeting part of your marital responsibility. This is fraudulent behavior. You are purposely depriving your mate of what they have a right to expect from you. If you have a problem fulfilling this aspect of your marriage covenant, then you should seek counsel. The King James translation of 1 Corinthians 7:5 reads:

> **Defraud ye not one the other, except it be with consent for a time, that ye may give yourselves to fasting and prayer; and come together again, that Satan tempt you not for your incontinency.**

What if your spouse says he or she desires to pray and fast once a month for twenty days? Unless you are prepared to agree, tell him or her to forget it. If one partner is in favor of prayer and fasting and the other is not, then the one in favor of prayer and fasting must still fulfill the marital obligation. Just because your mate says he or she is going to pray and fast, does not mean they can opt out of marital responsibility.

This type of situation would be like my wife deciding that she is going on a diet and does not want to be tempted by cooking food. Well, this is fine for her, but what about the children and me? She still needs to cook for us. Therefore, it is reasonable to expect her to consider the needs of her family. Of course, as a concerned husband, I would also want to consider what I might otherwise be able to do to help my wife meet her goal of losing weight. What makes her happy ultimately makes me happy — and vice versa.

Your situation may be different. You may be married to a person who is involved in drugs. Your spouse may be so committed to drugs that he or she comes home all worn out and unable to fulfill the marital relationship in an intimate, physical manner. (Actually, it is not safe to be intimate with someone who is on drugs, so I would advise against it.) In this case, your spouse is defrauding you by depriving you. Regardless of the reason, if one partner is not fulfilling his or her responsibilities, a door is open for trouble.

Physical intimacy is such a need within a marriage that 1 Corinthians 7:10-11 says the woman should not leave or separate from her husband. Nor should the man separate from his wife.

Now to the married I command, yet not I but the Lord: A wife is not to depart from her husband.

But even if she does depart, let her remain unmarried or be reconciled to her husband. And a husband is not to divorce his wife.

Yet, this Scripture does say, **But even if she does depart.** This suggests there are indeed times you may have to put some space between you and the person you married. The Spirit of God would never have inspired Paul to add the conjunction *but* to his declaration if separation was unconditionally impermissible in the eyes of God.

Resolving Issues Through Separation

There are instances when separation is appropriate. Separation is often the only realistic option when drug abuse has become a serious issue. Addicts often are more committed to getting high than to the person they married. Drugs manipulate the addict's actions, drain their money, and absorb all their time and attention. Drugs rob the addict of the ability to make right decisions.

The Second Choice: Separation

If your spouse is taking drugs and not bringing home his or her weekly paycheck, this deserves your immediate attention. If your spouse begins carrying off things from your home to sell for drugs, it is not time to hope and pray that things will get better. It's time to take action. Wisdom dictates separation to protect yourself, your children, and your home.

Such issues as pornography, physical and verbal abuse, or failure to financially support the family may also be resolved through a separation. Some spouses are caught up in watching sexually explicit pornography and desire to bring these activities into their bedrooms. Pornography invites feelings of betrayal into a relationship. Injured spouses often find that they are not able to stay committed to sexual intimacy because they cannot be sure if their mate is thinking about them or someone else during sex. Complications arise once their spouse expects them to act like the "Ultimate Lover" on the video screen. Do not be naïve; there is a serious problem in the relationship.

When I was in Bible school and worked in a convenience store, one evening I noticed this guy standing in the corner flipping through the porno magazines. He invited me to look at one of the pages he was leering at.

"I'm not going to look at that," I said.

"What's wrong?" he questioned.

"I just recognize that God did not make that woman to be lusted after and abused like that," I told him.

Then I asked him, "By the way, are you married?"

"Yes," he answered.

"Doesn't it seem strange that you are getting turned on by a magazine when you have the real thing waiting for you at home?" I asked.

Needless to say, he did not buy the magazine. Why? Because I appealed to his reasoning. But, there are some people who do not care how much reason you appeal to. They are going to get their porno turn-on anyway, and they want to be left alone so they can go in the alley and have what they think is a good time. Then they will go home and fall asleep next to their spouse. Sometimes separation is necessary to bring such people to their senses and to bring about reconciliation and mutual fulfillment.

Spouses are to enjoy physical intimacy together; pornography is an intrusion. If the "Ultimate Lover" is occupying your spouse's attention, then you need to communicate that you are within your biblical rights not to participate as a partner. You need to tell your spouse: "If you want to be sexually excited or gratified by that junk, then I will withhold the real thing! If you want our relationship to work, let's get marriage counseling."

Some people have been given the impression that they have to stay with an abusive spouse no matter what. "I've always heard that since you've made your bed, you have to lie in it," they will say. This is sheer foolishness. The latter part of 1 Corinthians 7:15 says you have been called to peace.

It is not wise to stay in such an environment. Do you want your daughter to grow up and marry a man who treats her without respect? Do you want your son to grow up thinking that being a man means physically or mentally abusing his wife, just like he saw Daddy do? This happens in far too many cases and perpetuates the problem. If your spouse is beating you and you fail to take responsible action, you are setting the stage for disaster.

Finally, I have had women come to me saying, "Pastor, my husband is not bringing home any money." Well, if he is not bringing in any money, then wisdom dictates you take some course of action. Second Thessalonians 3:10 says, **If anyone will not work, neither shall he eat.**

In 1 Corinthians 7:12-14, the Bible speaks of your spouse being "willing to live" with you. The King James Version translates "willing to live" as being "pleased to dwell with." I prefer the King James translation because I believe it to be more accurate. Look at how this entire passage of Scripture was originally translated in the King James Version:

> **But to the rest speak I, not the Lord: If any brother hath a wife that believeth not, and she be pleased to dwell with him, let him not put her away.**
>
> **And the woman which hath an husband that believeth not, and if he be pleased to dwell with her, let her not leave him.**
>
> **For the unbelieving husband is sanctified by the wife, and the unbelieving wife is sanctified by the husband: else were your children unclean; but now they are holy.**
>
> **But if the unbelieving depart, let him depart. A brother or a sister is not under bondage in such cases: but God hath called us to peace.**

We are to have peace in our relationships. And this peace only comes when both spouses **are pleased to dwell with each other**, as the King James Version says — not just *willing to live together*. Why? You can be *willing* to live with someone because of your circumstances and yet not be very pleased about it.

Now, if your spouse is taking the household money and consuming it with drinking and parties and your family is suffering, then how can he or she be showing commitment? The normal conclusion is that your spouse must not be *pleased to dwell with* you. If your partner is physically abusive or talks about you like dirt, then such a spouse must not be *pleased to dwell with you.* If your husband or wife is treating your children without love, he or she is not *pleased to dwell with you.* If your spouse prefers the physical stimulation of pornography to real intimacy with you, or pursues an indulgence in drugs rather than a normal home life, this person is not *pleased to dwell with you.* Some kind of godly change is needed. Recognize that you do not have to stay in that kind of relationship. You have options, and the first alternative to tolerating that condition — after you have tried to work out in a loving and supportive way the problems that have beset your partnership — is to separate.

Can I Be With Someone Else?

Separation is a godly option in that it can bring about reconciliation and a happy and fulfilling marital relationship. So, dating someone else obviously would be counterproductive.

Separation is not a time to get involved in another relationship. Your desire is to be set on the hope of reconciling with your mate and developing a truly prosperous marriage. This is why Paul declares in 1 Corinthians 7:11 that if a wife departs or separates from her husband, she is to remain unmarried or be reconciled to her husband — not go out and look for someone else. The same is true for the husband.

But how can you be *unmarried* if you are only separated from your spouse? Well, the seventh chapter of 1 Corinthians goes on to explain in verse 34:

> **There is a difference between a wife and a virgin. The unmarried woman cares about the things of the Lord, that she may be holy both in body and in spirit. But she who is married cares about the things of the world — how she may please her husband.**

What Paul means is that a spouse who is separated is to act as if he or she is single and committed to being holy in both body and spirit, doing the will of God. In other words, the attention of the spouse who departs from the marital relationship is to be directed toward God. **Let her** (him) **remain unmarried,** means acting like a woman (or a man) who is a virgin and committed to doing the will of God. A person who is separated should not be on the prowl. They are not free to act like a single person considering marriage.

"But, what if I am asked out on a date while my spouse and I are separated?" Well, what about it? What does another person's advances have to do with the fact that you are married and have made a vow to be solely committed to your mate? If you choose to separate and want to be right with God, then your commitment to working out your marriage must be true. Otherwise, there is no real chance of your present marital relationship working out. You may be fooling your spouse, your family, others, and even yourself, but you are not fooling God.

How you conduct yourself in these situations reveals whether or not you are truly committed to seeing your marriage succeed. You need to be honest with yourself. As a person who has been very happily married for almost 20 years, I must tell you that every marriage experiences challenges. And at these times of challenge, the other grass always looks greener. If you do not see this deception for what it is, then you could end up doing permanent damage to your marriage.

What if My Spouse Is an Unbeliever?

First Corinthians 7:12-14 answers this question very plainly:

> **But to the rest I, not the Lord, say: If any brother has a wife who does not believe, and she is willing to live with him, let him not divorce her.**
>
> **And a woman who has a husband who doesn't believe, if he is willing to live with her, let her not divorce him.**
>
> **For the unbelieving husband is sanctified by the wife, and the unbelieving wife is sanctified by the husband; otherwise your children would be unclean, but now they are holy.**

So whether your spouse is a Believer or not has no bearing on your obligation to your marriage covenant. Paul expressly says let him not divorce her and let her not divorce him, providing she is willing to live with him and he is willing to live with her.

Actually, I like the way the traditional King James translates this passage:

But to the rest speak I, not the Lord: If any brother hath a wife that believeth not, and she be pleased to dwell with him, let him not put her away.

And the woman which hath a husband that believeth not, and if he be pleased to dwell with her, let her not leave him.

For the unbelieving husband is sanctified by the wife, and the unbelieving wife is sanctified by the husband; else were your children unclean; but now they are holy.

Where the New King James says **let him not divorce her** and **let her not divorce him,** the traditional King James reads **let him not put her away** and **let her not leave him.** I believe the traditional King James is a better translation. Why? Because in the original Greek text, the same words — **Let him not put her [him] away** — are used in referring to both the husband staying with his wife and the wife staying with her husband. This Greek word is *aphiemi;* sometimes spelled as *afienai.* Strong's Exhaustive Concordance says the meaning of *aphiemi* is "to send forth," as in to leave, let (alone), or put (send) away. *Aphiemi* comes from the Greek prefix *apo* and Greek root word *hiemi.* Strong's says *apo* denotes separation, while *hiemi* means, "to send from." Although you could interpret *aphiemi* to mean "divorce" or "to get a divorce," the meaning of the original Greek indicates that "separation" or "to separate," as is reflected in the King James translation, is a more accurate translation.

With this in mind, you can now see more clearly the spirit of what Paul was telling the Church at Corinth. First Corinthians

7:12-15 is saying that a husband or wife should not separate for just any cause, and the fact that your spouse is an unbeliever is not a proper reason to separate as long as the marriage partner is **pleased to dwell with you.** Why? Because if your unsaved spouse is **pleased to dwell with you** and you are living right, you will be a bright light to your mate. Your light can draw your spouse to receive Jesus; then your children will not be deprived of having both their parents.

As long as your spouse does not have a problem with your relationship with Jesus Christ, with you going to Bible Study and attending church, then you are not to separate. Even if your spouse says "Don't preach or talk to me about going to church," this is not grounds for separation. If your spouse is truly **pleased to dwell with you,** then he or she will see that Jesus has made you a better partner. It will not be long before your mate starts thinking, "Maybe I need to come to know Jesus like my spouse does."

Do not seek a way out of your marriage covenant; seek the way to making the most of what you have invested in your mate. If you separate yourself from your spouse who is *pleased to dwell with you* just because he or she is an unbeliever, it brings unnecessary reproach upon your commitment to Christ. First Corinthians 7:14 assures that the marriage relationship is right in the eyes of God, for it says that acceptance of Jesus Christ as Lord and Savior sanctifies the spouse and renders the children holy. Besides, how can you possibly determine that your spouse is no longer capable of being a good partner just because you have accepted Jesus Christ as your personal Lord and Savior?

Now, verses 12 and 13 of 1 Corinthians chapter 7 expressly say, **if he** (or she) **is pleased to dwell with her** (or him) they should stay together. The word *if* is conditional. This is the criterion that needs to be met.

What if My Mate Wants to Leave?

While their discontented spouse is dragging them across the floor in their effort to leave, some hold on, screaming, "I'm believing God for our marriage to be restored. Please stay!" If your mate does not want to dwell with you, you cannot override their displeasure with your faith.

Now, you may say, "Well, I'm just going to be patient and wait." All right, look at it this way: You were 22 when you got married. Now you are 32 and still waiting for your spouse to work out the problems that disrupt your marriage. It should be clear where your life is headed.

First Corinthians 7:15 specifically tells you:

But if the unbeliever departs, let him depart; a brother or a sister is not under bondage in such cases.

But God has called us to peace.

God has given you His assurance that He does not expect you to go through life trying to stay married to someone who does not want to be your spouse. If they want to leave, let them. The Lord will no longer consider you bound to an unbelieving spouse who leaves the marriage. Nor will He hold you accountable as the cause of the divorce.

In fact, if you try to get your spouse to remain without a change in heart toward God or a change in their evil actions toward you, then your own efforts are suspect. First

IS DIVORCE A SIN?

Corinthians 7:15 says to let go of a spouse who is determined to go, because you have been called to peace.

"But Pastor, my spouse is a Believer and wants to leave
me and our children." Well, if your spouse refuses to live
according to God's Word, then he or she is acting like an
unbeliever. Am I right? Jesus said those who hear and
actually do His Word are His disciples indeed. So if your
spouse leaves your marriage, it is as the departing of an
unbeliever. In other words, you are no longer to perform
nuptial responsibilities.

Look at how this verse ends. It declares that **God has
called us to peace**. This tells me that if you should come to
the point where you must divorce your spouse in order to
have peace in your home, you can still expect to be blessed
with an abundant life in Christ Jesus. Believe God, and He
will give you another mate who will love you as Christ loves
the Church (Ephesians 5:25). Jesus loved the Church so
much that He gave His life for it. He was consumed with
fulfilling the needs of His Church. In the meantime, your
heavenly Father will provide everything you need
(Philippians 4:19), because you have trusted in Him enough
to reach out for His very best.

How Long Should a Separation Be?

"I'm waiting for my spouse to come back to me," one
woman says.

"How long has he been gone?" I ask.

"Fifteen years."

"Are you divorced?" I asked, puzzled.

"No, I'm separated."

36

Now I have one last question: "Do you know you are contributing to your spouse's sin?"

If you and your spouse have been separated over a period of years and your spouse has engaged in sex with someone other than you, your spouse is committing adultery and you are accountable. Whatever your spouse does automatically affects you because you are still tied together as one.

Too many Christians decide to remain separated indefinitely when trouble challenges their marriages, rather than to deal with the challenges head-on. Some have separated for as many as five, ten, and even twenty years. Eventually they become frustrated, unhappy, and miserable because they cannot really share their lives with anyone else. This is not of God. What kind of witness are they able to be for the Lord? Obviously, they do not realize that the Lord cannot bring them into a positive relationship because they are still another person's spouse. Besides that, they are contributing to sin by allowing the possibility of their spouse entering an adulterous relationship because they have not brought finality to their marriage. If God were to really bless such a relationship, then wouldn't He be condoning their disobedient behavior? You need to go on with your life, especially if your spouse is set on being physically intimate with other people. Say to yourself: "I'm going to go on and walk with God. I am going to bring closure to this relationship so God can bless me with someone who will follow His order for marriage."

My Mate Needs Help

Remaining in an abusive relationship can be detrimental to your health, as well as to your children's health. The courts understand this; if a man is abusive, they will come and take him away. The courts will intervene because they recognize that spousal abuse can cause grave bodily harm, and it can be reasonable cause for separation and even divorce. You need to be just as wise.

If you are married to a chronic drug user, it is unlikely that he or she will submit to counseling if no one takes the steps necessary to make them aware of the severity of their condition. It is up to you to bring this issue out into the open and to force your spouse to deal with the problem head-on. You must let your spouse know that there has to be a change. Otherwise, you give consent to your spouse's failure to come to terms with what is destroying the marriage and quite possibly their life.

Here's what to say to such a spouse: "You have a drug problem. There are drug rehabilitation programs, and I would like you to enter one. I will come visit and be there for you while you are getting help and recovering. But I am also going to be monitoring your progress while you are getting sober. I am committed to helping you, just as long as you are committed too. But know that I will be paying attention to how your recovery is coming along."

It is essential that you spell out your reasoning for, and the terms of, your separation before you physically separate. No matter how basic and obvious the issues may seem, you must not forget that your spouse is blinded by his or her problem. So what is obvious to you will not be as obvious to him or her until you begin to talk about it.

The Importance of Predetermined Issues

You never want to separate unless you both know the issues and conditions. If you do not know what the issues are, how can you expect to know if the separation has worked?

Say your spouse has this crass attitude: "I want you to warm up my bed at night, yet I'm going to treat you like a dog." Well, separation is intended to get the attention of the disrespectful spouse. So when you are not there to warm the bed, your spouse is going to realize that something is radically wrong. But how is your mate going to know what the problem is?

This is why you need to predetermine the issues. You cannot expect any progress toward overcoming your challenges when the issues have not been clearly defined. You have to say to your spouse, "The way you treat me is a problem." If you say, "Well, I just cannot explain it," then you cannot expect your spouse to think much of the problem. Your spouse needs to know the way you think the marriage ought to be. If they know, maybe things will be different. Maybe what you think is not realistic, but how are you going to know if you both do not talk and use God's Word as your standard? It is extremely important to openly discuss the issues troubling your marriage *before* you separate.

You also need to discuss the parameters of your separation. While affirming your commitment to seeing your relationship through this rough time, tell your spouse that you are placing some limitations on him or her to protect what the two of you have left. For example, you might say that your home and property are off-limits, and that you will not be having intimate relations until certain issues are properly resolved. You might add: "I'm serious about making a change in our relationship, so I am going to watch and see if you are just as serious about making our marriage work by the way you treat me and our children." This way, you let your spouse know that his or her destructive habits are not going to continue. You must be prepared to follow through on your word.

There also needs to be a recording of the issues and the terms so that there is no room for confusion once you have parted. Often the spouse who has been acting ungodly will come back claiming that this or that was or was not said. Writing down the issues and conditions helps to keep the separation on target and enables you to determine if and when it is successful. Now you are in better position to follow through on your word because you know, without a shadow of a doubt, what you have agreed to. If you do not write down the issues, it will be next to impossible for your separation to be truly effective once confusion and manipulation set in.

Use the time before you separate to express your hope that your spouse will want again what you had before. Regardless of the issues causing a division between you and your spouse, your underlying message must clearly tell them that you want the relationship to work.

Set a Goal for Reconciliation

The good news is that you can have a positive separation. But the only way the best is going to come is if you not only have predetermined issues and conditions for reconciliation, but set some goals and recommendations for meeting these goals.

For example, sharing with your spouse a clearly defined mental picture or image of how you desire your relationship to be is certainly a step in the right direction. But you need to be sure that what you desire is in line with God's Word; otherwise, you have no guarantee that it is truly possible. If your spouse has any desires for your future as a couple, be open to what he or she has to say and be willing to discuss any issues raised. Encourage your spouse to talk with you.

Once you have shared your desires, you then need to discuss and establish some possible goals and means of reaching them. If you cannot think of any practical ways to reach these goals, then resubmit your goals to the Word of God. In other words, is what you are wanting in your marriage realistic and right in terms of what God's Word has to say about marriage and the part that you and your spouse have to play in making your marriage blissful? Oftentimes, marriage partners are expecting to receive from their mate what they ultimately can only receive from God; they are looking to their mate to fulfill in them what only God can fulfill. Or, they are expecting their mate to carry the majority of the responsibility for the success of their marriage while they just simply enjoy all the benefits. Marriage doesn't work this way — it takes conscious effort on the part of both partners.

Be sure to write down the realistic goals you have established, along with an explanation of how you plan to achieve them. Record everything that you have agreed upon, if any agreement is indeed possible. You may have to simply record what you want, what the issues are, and what you intend to do about them.

In Habakkuk 2:2, the Lord instructed the prophet to write the vision and make it plain in order that it could be followed. In Deuteronomy 11:18, the Lord instructed His

41

people to keep His Words before their very eyes. Why? Because whatever you look at and focus on is what you eventually are going to do and achieve.

Only after you have discussed and recorded the issues relating to your separation, provided some possible solutions, and expressed your desired goals, along with your ideal for marriage, can a separation can be really effective and meaningful. Now both you and your spouse know what needs to be done to resolve the issues separating you. You have eliminated confusion. When you follow these simple guidelines before separating, it proves to be one of the most effective means of letting the spouse who is not committed to living according to the Word of God know that you mean business.

No predetermined issues and goals usually results in no plans being made to correct what is challenging your marriage. No plans usually makes for no solutions. Yet, challenges with dealing honestly, communicating, respect, faithfulness, and fidelity are important issues that can be resolved if your desires are clarified beforehand and realistic goals for improvement are set.

If communication is an issue that needs to be addressed, you can suggest: "Let's make an agreement that every Wednesday and Friday night we will talk between such and such a time. If you do not call me, then I know you really do not want to improve our communication."

This tables the issue and sets a goal for communicating with one another. So, now you have a way of monitoring whether your separation is truly working, because you have predetermined the issues, stated what you want, and taken the first steps to resolving this issue and achieving your goals. You always want to set goals so that you are able to monitor progress.

The Second Choice: Separation

When you separate with predetermined issues and goals, you are saying to your spouse, "Here are the problem(s), and here are our goals. Let's give ourselves such and such time totally apart from each other to achieve these goals. Let us see what it is like without each other. We will not be together in a physical way for a certain period of time." Make it plain and be sure to tell your spouse: "This separation is not because I want to go out and be with someone else, but so we can see that we are better off together than apart."

If your spouse is determined not to get any help or thinks, "I don't need to change; there is nothing wrong with me," then you must make a decision. If your spouse continues to want to beat you or is still disrespectful, then you need to seek what God's will is for you concerning this marital relationship. You may have to let your spouse know that you are willing to divorce, but this should be your last option.

The Importance of Time Constraints

And finally, you never want to separate for an indefinite period of time. Why? First of all, 1 Corinthians 7:5 tells you that Satan will come in at a restraint or a ceasing of intimate marital relations. He is a tempter, and he will take every opportunity to challenge your marital relationship. This means you will have problems if your separation drags out. Secondly, how are you going to know when your separation has run its course if you don't set a time limit? How will your spouse know that you are truly serious about wanting and needing a change? Thirdly, when you separate for an indefinite period of time, it is going to work against you because you are compounding a bad situation with an even worse one. You are now trading uncertainty for even more uncertainty.

If your spouse fails to make any promising changes in his or her actions towards you and your family within a reasonable amount of time, then you have a right to say, "If you want to go on as you are, fine. But you are not going to stop me and our children from moving on to a better life."

You never ever go into a separation saying, "Well, we will just separate until." Until when? Until what? I will tell you what is going to happen — you will see the negative side of separation. Your spouse, who is not committed to treating you right, is going to do all the things he or she thinks is fun while you are trying to do what is right. You will have indefinitely put your life on hold while experiencing the desires of a married person whose needs are unfulfilled.

If you have predetermined a time constraint and a means of monitoring the progress of your separation, you can calm your body and mind in times of great temptation. You can say, "Well, in so many weeks we will see if this relationship is going to work out. If it is not working out, then I am going to end this relationship and go on. Body, just be patient!" If your separation is working out, then you can say to your body, "Our separation is working out really well and things are heading toward being the way God meant for them to be. This separation is going to bring about a positive marriage. So be patient, body."

Without any predetermined goals and no means of monitoring the progress of your separation, you have no definite answer to use to assure yourself. The Bible even warns that this will happen if you do not come together in a physically intimate way as you should. In 1 Corinthians 7:5, the Scripture says not to:

> **...Deprive one another except with consent for a time, that you may give yourselves to fasting and prayer; and come together again so that Satan does not tempt you because of your lack of self-control.**

Fasting and prayer is a type of separation — one that is godly and mutually agreed upon. But, still, the Bible warns that this separation should only be for a time because of the possibility of your lack of self-control. The Bible is saying that after a period of time you will surely find yourself thinking, "Man, I have never been tempted like this before!"

Now, you may think, "I have always been faithful, so this would not be a problem for me." Well, you were always faithful back when you and your spouse were together and you had the opportunity of satisfying your physical urges. But now that you are separated and do not know when or even if you will be coming back together, others begin to look good.

I have had many people call and ask me, "Pastor, I have a friend at work and this person really enjoys going to lunch with me. I am having a challenge in my marriage, and I am separated. I want to go out with this person. He or she is really nice and has been helping me. In fact, he or she is even praying and believing God with me."

What do I say? I say, Cut it out! Why? Because you are hungry — and not for food either. The next thing you know, you will end up in a physically intimate relationship. How can I be so sure? There is a biblical principle that says

45

IS DIVORCE A SIN?

Everything looks edible; everything looks desirous to a hungry person.

Proverbs 27:6-8 confirms what 1 Corinthians 7:5 warns,

> **Faithful are the wounds of a friend, but the kisses of an enemy are deceitful.**
>
> **A satisfied soul loathes the honeycomb, but to a hungry soul every bitter thing is sweet.**
>
> **Like a bird that wanders from its nest, is a man who wanders from his place.**

If you have already separated from your mate without any predetermined time constraint, then you are undoubtedly already aware of this. You need to go back and set some time constraints on your separation.

I have known spouses who have left their marriage partner while screaming, "I hate you and I'll be back whenever!" This is not constructive. *Whenever* will never work to your advantage. Like it or not, realize it or not, you have just opened the door for someone else to take your place in your spouse's life. Without a time constraint, you will soon be asking your spouse, "When can I come home?" or "When will you come home?" And he or she will likely tell you, "I'll have to let you know." It is time to put all this nonproductive, illogical behavior behind you and your marriage.

Establishing predetermined time constraints sends a warning to your spouse. You are in essence telling him or her, "You get only so much time to get it together. These are the issues, here are the goals, and this is the opportunity to do something about them. At the end of this time, if these issues have not improved and we are not working on our goals together, then I am making another decision. All of your begging, crying, bawling, whining and saying how much you love me will not make any difference then. You can forget all of those dramatics. If you love me, here is your chance to prove it. I am giving you an opportunity now to do something about what is troubling our marriage. And you can be sure I am not going to let this drag out."

This is the attitude you must have when dealing with a spouse who is taking you for granted. If your spouse is not given the impression that you are serious, he or she will do little to make things right. Then, at the end of the final week of your predetermined time period, he or she will come to you begging, crying, and claiming to have changed. So you need to decide up-front: What if your spouse waits until the very last day and says he or she sees the light?

Here is something that should help you: Your mate had weeks — maybe months — to do something before this day arrived. Why has he or she not consistently gone to the rehabilitation program, attended counseling sessions, communicated with you, or done whatever it was that you discussed as possible solutions? If you were not a priority then, why are you such a priority now? And how long will you remain a priority?

You can rightfully say, "I forewarned you that if you did not begin to deal with the issues we discussed on a consistent and progressive basis, then I would consider other options. I gave you my word that I would support you in the changes that needed to be made, but you failed to take the initiative. You did not go through what needed to be done because you apparently were not serious. It seems to me that you did not really care. I have given you ample warning. It is time for me to move on."

Don't Be the Fall Guy

This may sound cold and harsh, but think of what your spouse has put you and your children through. Do you really want to continue dealing with issues that are tearing you and your children apart? Let me forewarn you: You cannot go back on your word and expect your spouse to respect you. A lack of accountability is part of what has brought trouble into your marriage. So strongly consider whether to give your negligent spouse another set of weeks to destroy your life. Do not let a bad situation drag out.

Recognize beforehand that when a spouse who is in disobedience is separated from the one who wants to turn their problems around, the spouse who is acting wrongly will often sidestep the issues by placing the blame on the partner who wants to do right. "I had to do something about my needs," the ungodly-acting spouse will reason. "You separated from me and the Bible says you are supposed to be a mate to me and that the marriage bed is undefiled. You left me with no other choice but to find someone else to take your place. I would not have had those affairs if you had been acting like the spouse you are supposed to be."

Suddenly, you are at fault for choosing to do right.

The next thing you are likely to hear from your spouse is, "I did not even know why you were leaving, or if you were coming back. You know I am a person with needs, so I had to have someone else take up where you left off." Suddenly, the issues that caused you to separate end up not being discussed because you have even greater troubles to consider, and you are the one being blamed. This is the type of game that an ungodly-acting spouse often plays.

Don't be the fall guy. Take the necessary precautions by laying out the issues, then setting goals and a time constraint.

The Biblical Way to Separate

First Corinthians 7:5 really is the key to how you should handle any form of separation. Although it is talking about giving yourself to fasting and prayer, the important thing to recognize is that fasting and prayer are a form of separation. Look at how the Word of God indicates that a separation is to be handled. First, by consent, which indicates that you and your spouse have talked about this separation first. Secondly, for a set time; a time constraint is agreed upon before the separation. Thirdly, this separation is about giving yourself to fasting and prayer, so a goal or purpose has been established. And finally, you are to come back together. This tells you what God intended as the objective of any separation. By following the example of how to separate found in 1 Corinthians 7:5, you protect yourself.

Yet, even in the very best scenarios, there is a negative side. Separation is not some magic cure-all. Its most negative aspects lie in the fact that there is a distance between you and your spouse. This distance is going to automatically hinder communication, which usually is enough of a challenge while you both are living under the same roof. So before you separate, you need to first realize that you are not going to be able to communicate with each other as you did when you were living together. This is why I highly recommend, in fact stress, that you talk to your spouse before you separate. Be sure you keep the lines of communication open by setting aside time to talk to each other while you are apart.

49

IS DIVORCE A SIN?

Also, the distance between you and your spouse is
going to require effort to bridge. I'm telling you right
now that you will have to go out of your way to make
your separation work; neither of you can expect the other
to make all the effort. Your spouse should be able to
depend on your support. If you are not willing to go out
of your way to work on your marriage, then forget about
separation; it's pointless.

Child care is another consideration. Have you asked
the Lord how you are supposed to explain to your children
the changes that are taking place within your family? You
need to prepare your children for what is to come. You need
to instill in them the assurance that things are going to get
better, that this separation is meant to bring about a positive
change. You need to assure them that you and your spouse
love them, and tell them that they can always ask questions
and talk about how they feel. Recognize that your children
will need extra time and attention throughout this separation. Then, you have to trust your children into the very
capable and loving hands of the Lord.

Never forget that your children have a vested interest in
your spouse, regardless of what happens in your marital relationship. Therefore, you will need to watch what you say
about your spouse in front of your children. Expressions of
anger, disappointment, and frustration will only serve as an
open door to instill a sense of insecurity in your children.
Follow these principles found in Philippians 4:8, and this
will help you to guard and control your mouth:

**Finally, brethren, whatever things are true,
whatever things are noble, whatever things are**

**just, whatever things are pure, whatever things
are lovely, whatever things are of good report, if
there is any virtue and if there is anything praise-
worthy; meditate on these things.**

There is also the issue of finances. Separation and divorce can drain the finances, especially if godly wisdom is
not used and you are not prepared to follow the Bible's di-
rections for ensuring the prosperity of your family. Do your
best to set your house in order, from a financial perspective,
before you separate. The Lord is willing to be your Provider, yet never forget that He expects you (James 1:5-7) to
be a wise steward.

When you know in your heart and by the Word of God
that you should separate from your spouse, do not stop seeking God. In other words, continue to follow the precedence
set in His Word. Ask the Lord the exact details of how and
when, and what you should do every step of the way. Remember that what you sense in your heart should line up
with what you read in your Bible. The Lord will never direct you to do something that is contrary to His Word.

If you do not continue to do what you know in your
heart that is confirmed in the Word of God, what began as a
step of faith could turn into an act of presumption and foolishness. Unfortunately, too many people start out in faith
and, through human reasoning and self-will, end up acting
foolish or presumptuously. Then, when the blessings of God
do not manifest, they doubt whether they made the right
decision to separate in the first place. They wonder if maybe
God wanted them to just tolerate the trouble in their marriage, when God's Word says the contrary.

51

IS DIVORCE A SIN?

Separation is obviously not a decision that should be taken lightly or made in haste. For separation to be a success, it will require much prayer and total submission to God throughout the entire time. If you enter a separation with your eyes on God, and keep your attention on Him, then you will end up the winner regardless of what happens. So, do not be discouraged. Proverbs 13:19 reminds you that **A desire accomplished is sweet to the soul.**

FOUR

THE THIRD CHOICE: DIVORCE

I had just flown in from Nagoya, Japan, and my wife had picked me up from the airport to whisk me away to the San Diego area for a honeymoon-type of excursion at a posh hotel. As we approached the hotel counter, the reservationist noticed the smiles on our faces. We informed her that we were on a romantic getaway since we had been apart from each other for nearly two weeks. We ended up talking about our relationship and how happy we were together, so I asked her if she was married as well. She replied that she was divorced and a single parent. Because my marriage has been such a blessing, I absent-mindedly expressed sorrow that her marriage had ended in a divorce. She quickly responded, "I'm not." She was smiling as she continued, "I have preserved a sane life for myself and my daughter. My husband was self-destructive. He was abusive, stealing from our home, and he was unfaithful. The best thing that I did for our relationship was to get a divorce."

Now, I should have known better than to say that I was sorry, because I know the Bible does not consider divorce to be wrong if used properly. According to the Scriptures, divorce is a solution, not a stigma. It is a form of redemption. Of course, there will always be those who misuse divorce, but this does not make divorce, in and of itself, wrong. In this woman's case, divorce was used properly, for it brought peace and restoration to her family.

Divorce is not God's best, but it is a way for you to go from victimization to victory. The Bible very clearly states that you should not go through life married to someone who does not want to be your spouse. God intended you to have a wonderful, peaceful, and fulfilling life as a married person. No one ever has the right to cause your life to be miserable, regardless of who they may be. So, divorce is not only permissible; it is sometimes warranted. Yet, in any case, it is not God's ideal.

Divorce is the dissolution of a marital relationship. In other words, the government of the land in which you live decrees that you are no longer married and therefore no longer responsible to each other. When this happens, God no longer holds you responsible for your former spouse, as ordered in Ephesians 5:22-33:

> **Wives, submit to your own husband as to the Lord. For the husband is head of the wife, as also Christ is head of the church; and He is the Savior of the body.**

Therefore, just as the church is subject to Christ, so let the wives be to their own husbands in everything.

Husbands, love your wives, just as Christ also loved the church and gave Himself for her,

That He might sanctify and cleanse her with the washing of water by the word,

That He might present her to Himself a glorious church, not having spot or wrinkle or any such thing, but that she should be holy and without blemish.

So husbands ought to love their own wives as their own bodies; he who loves his wife loves himself.

For no one ever hated his own flesh, but nourishes and cherishes it, just as the Lord does the church.

For we are members of His body, of his flesh and of His bones.

"For this reason a man shall leave his father and mother and be joined to his wife, and the two shall become one flesh."

This is a great mystery, but I speak concerning Christ and the church.

Nevertheless let each one of you in particular so love his own wife as himself, and let the wife see that she respects her husband.

Because the heavenly Father honors the government's decree, women are no longer obligated to respect and submit to their former husband. Neither are men required to love and care for their former wives as they do themselves.

IS DIVORCE A SIN?

In Deuteronomy 24:1-4, you can see exactly what a divorce entails from a biblical standpoint. This passage of Scripture lets you know that a written certificate of divorce must be given and that the couple must cease living together and having sexual relations. Only then is a marriage truly terminated in the eyes of God.

> **"When a man takes a wife and marries her, and it happens that she finds no favor in his eyes because he has found some uncleanness in her, and he writes her a certificate of divorce, puts it in her hand, and sends her out of his house,**
>
> **"When she has departed from his house, and goes and becomes another man's wife..."**

The next verses continue:

> **"If the latter husband detests her and writes her a certificate of divorce, puts it in her hand, and sends her out of his house, or if the latter husband dies who took her as his wife,**
>
> **"Then her former husband who divorced her must not take her back to be his wife after she has been defiled; for that is an abomination before the LORD, and you shall not bring sin on the land which the LORD your God is giving you as an inheritance."**

The last verse indicates that once the certificate of divorce is received and the couple separates from each other, the two cannot go back to each other as if they are still married. They cannot resume their former relationship.

Now, before God had given the children of Israel His Law concerning divorce, they did not have any such practice. When a man was displeased with his wife, he simply separated her from himself and either took a new wife or called for one of his other wives. The idea of giving your spouse with whom you are displeased a certificate of divorce was instituted by God. God had Moses give the Law to the children of Israel. Therefore, divorce — in and of itself — obviously cannot be a sin, because God instructs His people in righteousness, not unrighteousness (2 Timothy 3:16).

To sin means to transgress God's will, or we can say in today's vernacular to "miss the mark," as in missing the bull's-eye. If your marriage has ended, or seems to be ending in a divorce, somewhere along the way one or both of you must have missed your target. So, the actual sin was the behavior that led to divorce, not the divorce — at least that's the way Jesus, the Son of God, sees it. Jesus is recorded in both Matthew 19:8 and Mark 10:5 as saying that it was because of the hardness of man's heart that divorce was instituted.

Don't you think that God knows a person can be hardhearted about drugs or pornography? God knows some men are hardhearted about staying out and never coming home at a decent hour. Likewise, He knows that a woman may want to party and stay out with her friends. The Lord knows a person's heart can become hard toward their mate, and this is what He sees as the sin — not the act of getting a divorce. Divorce is simply the means to redeem those who are tied through marital bonds to a hardhearted person. Therefore, divorce is permissible in the eyes of God — not desirable, but permissible.

Unfortunately, far too many people have the impression that divorce is an unpardonable sin. They think it is better to stay bound in an unhealthy relationship than to put an end to marital abuse by means of a divorce. This is in direct contrast to the redemptive nature of the heavenly Father and could not be further from the truth. There is only one unpardonable sin and that is rejecting, or not accepting, Jesus Christ as your personal Lord and Savior (Mark 3:28-29). This alone is the unpardonable sin because Acts 4:12 says:

> **"Nor is there salvation in any other, for there is no other name under heaven given among men by which we must be saved."**

Since it is only by Jesus that you can be saved, you have no other way to be free of — or pardoned for — sin. But once you accept Jesus Christ as your personal Lord and Savior, you are automatically delivered from any sin and have a right to forgiveness for any you may commit thereafter. First John 1:9 says:

> **If we confess our sins, He is faithful and just to forgive us our sins and to cleanse us from all unrighteousness.**

So, even if divorce, in and of itself, were a sin, it could not be an unpardonable sin because of the redemption available in Christ Jesus. All you would have to do is confess that you made a mistake, and you have God's Word that you would be pardoned.

It is particularly important to see that divorce is not an unpardonable sin if you are involved in an abusive marital relationship. Maybe you believe you have to let your spouse have access to your home, even though he or she is selling everything you own to buy drugs or is having sexual encounters while you are away. Maybe you think, "My spouse is into pornography, and I have to put up with it because I can't get divorced and still be right with God." Well, through the Scripture, God is telling you that if your spouse is doing you wrong, then you have His permission to divorce, even if he or she does not want you to leave.

I make this point because the person with a hard heart usually wants the spouse to stay around and keep taking the abuse. He or she may even try to make the spouse feel guilt and condemnation. This is not of God; Romans 8:1 says:

> **There is now no condemnation to those who are in Christ Jesus, who do not walk according to the flesh** [like the spouse with a hard heart], **but according to the spirit.**

If your spouse wants to keep you as a victim, if he or she wants to keep abusing and misusing you and does not appreciate you, then God says you are permitted to issue a certificate of divorce and leave.

God knew long before you got here that some people would refuse to acknowledge and live according to the truth. After all, there are those who refuse to accept Jesus the Christ as their personal Lord and Savior. Some people simply have hard hearts. And if they have a hard heart toward Jesus, who extends His unconditional love to them and who died for them, just imagine what their heart are like toward you.

You do not always know what you are getting into when you agree to marry, especially if you do not know the Word of God and have not been taught how to properly discern the Lord's voice. You can love the Lord with all your heart, even go to church and read the Bible, yet still make a bad decision and marry the wrong person. No one is perfect. Unfortunately, life can then become a type of hell on earth for you, even though Jesus came to provide you with an abundant life. This is why 1 Corinthians 7:15 says that if your spouse is not pleased to dwell with you, let them go — especially if he or she desires to depart. The Word of God says you are not bound to your marriage covenant in such cases.

Divorce Is Redemptive

Divorce, in and of itself, is redemptive. Think about it realistically. Divorce ends contention. It brings peace to one who has been tormented by the bad actions of an abusive spouse. It enables such a spouse to be free to go on and grow, while leaving the abusive one to deal with the consequences of his or her abuse. Divorce permits the innocent children to live in peace, free of strife and confusion.

Say you are a woman and your husband is not working. He tells you to go out and work while he lies around at home. You have tried separating from him, but he still manages to take your money. Well, your spouse is in disobedience. Genesis 2:15 says the Lord God took the man, whom He had formed of the dust of the ground and breathed the breath of life into, put him in the garden of Eden and told him to tend and keep it. In other words, the man was to work. So the man who does not work is going against what God designed him to do. Even if this man has accepted Jesus Christ as Lord and Savior and therefore has some relationship with the Lord, at the very least he has broken his fellowship with God through his disobedience.

Look at what the Spirit of the Lord says about such a man. In 1 Timothy 5:8, the King James translation tells you:

But if any provide not for his own, and especially for those of his own house, he hath denied the faith, and is worse than an infidel.

In 2 Thessalonians 3:10, in the New King James translation says you should not even feed him:

For even when we were with you, we commanded you this: If anyone will not work, neither shall he eat.

The Word of God says to let such a man become dissipated. This tells you how serious God is about a man fulfilling his God-given purpose in life. So, you have grounds for a divorce.

In reading the Scripture, you can see that Adam worked at tilling the soil before he was given Eve. This says to me that, like Adam, a man should not marry until he is first working. After all, Adam had gold, rubies, silver, diamonds, emeralds, and land, yet he still worked to such a degree that God had to tell him that on the seventh day that he was to rest (Genesis 2:2). Obviously, Adam was not working just to make ends meet; Adam worked because he was created to work. In fact, this Scripture reveals that men innately have such a strong propensity to work that often their wives have to remind them to come home.

If you are the wife of a man who refuses to work, then your spouse is not living the way God intended. Providing for him is only enabling him to defy what the Lord has ordained, and you are, in legal terms, abetting his crime. Cases like this illustrate how staying with a spouse who has a hard heart toward God can put you in the position of being an "enabler." In other words, your love, concern, and willingness to be responsible *enable* your spouse to continue doing what is not right in the eyes of God. God never intended for you to be a co-dependent, as it is called in certain rehabilitation programs. Being a co-dependent is not what the Lord meant by describing the woman as the man's *help meet*, as the King James translation says in Genesis 2:18. The woman was made to help a man do what God ordained him to do — not to enable him to do wrong! The very nature of divorce usually puts an end to co-dependency within a marriage.

Now, say you have put your entire life on hold because you married the wrong person. You ended up marrying Attila the Hun and Genghis Khan all wrapped up into one. Not until after you were married did you realize that your spouse did not really love you at all. Maybe you discovered that your spouse has another lover.

Your spouse is not necessarily going to change; he or she was that way before you were married. Your spouse may even have been bold and brash enough to tell you out-right to forget about anything changing. If you stay with such a spouse and allow your love to be violated, you leave yourself open to all sorts of sexually transmitted diseases, as well as all sorts of mental and physical abuse.

You have a decision to make. The Word of God says you can divorce. A divorce will redeem you from bondage to a spouse who is not willing to treat you right. You do not have to live in misery.

Just as divorce can put an end to a mistake, to deceit, and even to co-dependency, it can also be an act of mercy. Say you are married to a person who does not want to remain married to you. This desire to depart may or may not have anything to do with you. Is it not compassionate, loving, and kind to release your spouse from the marriage vow so you can both be happy? Why do you even want to be with someone who does not want to be with you? Releasing your spouse can be the steppingstone to a wonderful life with someone else who really values you.

Obviously, divorce is also a means of protection when one spouse is physically violent and refuses to seek rehabilitation. Even the government recognizes this.

Divorce can also be an act of protection when a spouse has broken the law, or foolishly jeopardized the safety and security of his or her family by getting involved with the wrong type of people. A divorce allows the innocent family members to get on with their lives.

God has called you to peace in your marriage, not confusion, violence, and strife. If you are in an abusive relationship that has stolen the peace of your family, a divorce frees you to make another home for yourself where you and your children can enjoy peace, safety, and security. Divorce provides the opportunity for your children to recover from the negative influences and consequences they have experienced as a part of your troubled marriage. In this sound environment, your children will be free and open to being taught as God has promised in Isaiah 54:13. Of course, divorce is not God's best, but it can free His people to achieve His best.

IS DIVORCE A SIN?

Now, if I were a betting man, I would wager that a disrespectful, dishonest, foolish, and disobedient spouse believes that, since you are a Christian, you should never get a divorce. In fact, I would not be the least bit surprised if your hardhearted partner has said to you, "You know, Jesus hates divorce." This is why it pays to know the Word of God and the character of your heavenly Father. Otherwise, your desire to do right and live right before God can be manipulated and used against you.

I have taken the time to show you that divorce cannot be a sin, and I have given you some scenarios for troubled marriages that qualify for divorce in the eyes of God. You should now be able to discern how the Word of God may apply to your particular situation. Even if none of these scenarios exactly fits your dilemma, you should be able to see that God wants your married life to be beneficial to you, rather than a means of hurt, harm, and detriment.

God instituted the certificate of divorce to ensure the possibility of an abundant life to those who obey His Word. But, I must warn you not to take God's mercy for granted. *The Lord did not institute divorce just so you would not have to stick with your spouse when a challenge arises.* Nor did God permit divorce so you could go pursue Miss Pretty or Mr. Handsome, who you now think would be a better catch than your spouse. Boredom in your marriage is not a viable excuse for divorce either. You can do something about being bored. None of these reasons is, or has ever been, why God permitted divorce.

May I Marry Someone Else?

In the Old Testament, Moses outlined the law of God concerning divorce for the children of Israel in Deuteronomy 24:1-4. The first two verses say:

> **"When a man takes a wife and marries her, and it happens that she finds no favor in his eyes because he has found some uncleanness in her, and he writes her a certificate of divorce, puts it in her hand, and sends her out of his house,**
>
> **"when she has departed from his house, and goes and becomes another man's wife..."**

Stop right there for a moment. Obviously, it must be permissible in the eyes of God for a divorced spouse to remarry; after all, the second verse says, "and goes and becomes another man's wife."

However, there are some prerequisites you must first fulfill. The first verse says that a certificate of divorce must be written and given, and then the two must physically separate themselves from each other. Apparently, giving a written certificate of divorce is different from putting away a spouse. Otherwise, why would the Law have commanded the children of Israel to both *write a certificate of divorce* and *to put away* the spouse? So, there are two different requirements to legally terminating your marriage.

If your spouse gives you a certificate of divorce, then you are free to marry someone else *after* you have physically separated. The same is true if you were the one to write a certificate of divorce. Once you or your spouse have left, you are free to marry someone else.

IS DIVORCE A SIN?

"But wait a minute, Pastor, Jesus said in Matthew 19:9 that:

'**Whoever divorces his wife, except for sexual immorality, and marries another, commits adultery; and whoever marries her who is divorced commits adultery.**'"

You are absolutely right — if you are reading the New King James Version (and, unfortunately, many other translations) of the Bible. However, I do not believe this was what Jesus actually said. In my studies, I have found that the original King James Version is a more accurate translation of what Jesus is saying. It quotes Jesus as telling His disciples:

'**Whosoever *shall put away* his wife, except it be for fornication, and shall marry another, committeth adultery: and whosoever marrieth her which is *put away* doth commit adultery.**'"

This translation says you are committing adultery if you marry another when you are only separated and have not brought an end to your marriage. Now, this lines up with what God said through Moses in Deuteronomy 24:1-4.

What accounts for the discrepancy between translations? Well, in the original Greek text, what is translated as *divorce* in the New King James Version and *put away* in the King James translation is the same Greek word "apolusai," a form of the Greek word "apoluo," meaning "to free fully, relieve, release, dismiss, let die, pardon or (let) depart, dismiss, divorce, forgive, let go, loose, put (send) away, release, set at liberty." The prefix *apo* by itself means "off" as in "away" and usually denotes separation, departure, cessation, completion, reversal. *Luo* is a primary verb meaning "to loosen, break (up), destroy, dissolve, put off." From this, you can see why some versions of the Bible translated the word "apolusai" (*"apoluo"*) as divorce rather than separation. However, when you read what Jesus is saying in light of its context within this passage of Scripture and the Old Testament Law, as well as the redemptive character of God, it becomes clear that Jesus could only be referring to what modern society calls separation.

I believe the proof of what I am saying lies within this passage of Scripture. In the seventh verse, the Pharisees confirm what the Lord God had ordained in Deuteronomy 24:1-4 by asking Jesus:

"Why then did Moses command to give a certificate of divorce and to put her away?"

What is translated as *certificate of divorce* in this Scripture is the Greek word "apostasiou," a form of the Greek word "apostasion." In the original text, it is the Greek word *apolusai* — to put away — that is found consistently throughout this passage of Matthew 19:3-10. In the third verse, when the Pharisees came to ask Jesus **"Is it lawful for a man to divorce his wife for just any reason?"** The Greek word translated as *divorce* is the word *apolusai*. In the eighth verse, when Jesus told the Pharisees, **"Moses, because of the hardness of your hearts, permitted you to divorce your wives..."** the Greek word for divorce is also *apolusai*. And in the ninth verse, when Jesus says **"Whoever divorces his wife, except for sexual immorality, and marries another, commits adultery; and whoever marries her who is divorced**

commits adultery" it is the Greek word *apolusai* that is translated as divorce.

Yet, in the seventh verse, when juxtaposed to certificate of divorce, *apolusai* is translated as "to put away" — as in *to separate* — in both the King James and the New King James translations. This tells me this Scripture is really talking about separation, not divorce.

The New Strong's Exhaustive Concordance of the Bible describes the Greek word *apostasiou* or *apostasion* as "something separative (spec) divorce (writing of) divorcement." A*postasiou* is a noun, whereas *apolusai* or *apolou* is a verb. So, in Matthew 19:7, the certificate of divorce is talking about a thing — the physical evidence of the spoken word. It is the decree or proclamation. On the other hand, *to put away* is the actual act of separation – the carrying out of this decree.

This Scripture is confirming that in order for your marriage to be ended in the eyes of God, you must do two things: Say it, with the evidence of giving it in writing, and then actually do it. This understanding of Matthew 19:10 falls right in line with the spiritual principle of faith. The procedure for ending a marital covenant relationship is the same as acting in faith: You have to say or confess it (make it known) and then you have to take corresponding action.

Also, why would Jesus confirm the Mosiac Law by saying in the eighth verse **"Moses, because of the hardness of your hearts, permitted you to divorce your wives..."** only to refute this by stating that **"Whoever divorces his wife and marries another commits adultery..."**? This does not make sense, nor does it concur with the character of God. First Corinthians 14:33 tells us that **God is not the**

author of confusion, and James 1:17 says **there is no variation or shadow of turning in God**. It would be contrary to the character of God to permit divorce in the Old Covenant and not in the New Covenant, which Hebrews 8:6 says is built upon better promises.

Now you may be thinking, "Then God lied when He spoke to Moses, because Jesus said in Matthew 19:8, **'But from the beginning it was not so...'**" Well, 1 Samuel 15:29 tells us that God cannot lie or relent, so Jesus was not saying that in the beginning divorce was prohibited, but was pointing out that this revelation from God had not yet been given to man. Why not? Apparently, it was not needed. The Lord does not waste the creative power of His Words. He does not give you what you do not need. God did not cover Adam and Eve with the skin of an animal until after they had sinned and realized they needed a covering (Genesis 3:21). The redemptive nature of God required that there be allowances for divorce in order to redeem an obedient spouse from bondage to the sin of a disobedient spouse.

All of this, I believe, shows that a more accurate or correct modern translation of what Jesus says in Matthew 19:9 would be:

> **"And I say to you, whoever separates from his or her spouse, except it be for adultery, and marries another, commits adultery; and whoever marries a spouse which is separated commits adultery."**

Jesus is saying that you are committing adultery if you are only separated from your spouse and you marry another person — or if you marry a person who is only separated from his or her spouse. Why? Because you are still technically married. In the United States, this is called bigamy. Bigamy is against state laws. You are violating both spiritual and natural human laws if you play around with bigamy.

What was really transpiring in Matthew 19 and Mark 10 was that the Pharisees were looking for a way to bring a reproach against Jesus. Since the Mosiac Law was highly regarded in their day, the Pharisees and Scribes sought to use their expert knowledge of the Law to discredit Jesus before the people.

Mark 10:2, in the King James Version of the Bible, records them asking Jesus, **"Is it lawful for a man to put away his wife?"** Knowing their true intentions, Jesus answered with a question: **"What did Moses command you?"** Of course, they were able to recite the Law for Jesus. They immediately responded in the fourth verse by saying that, **"Moses permitted a man to write a bill of divorcement and to put her away"** (KJV). Because their response was the truth, Jesus affirmed this.

If you read on in Mark's Gospel, you will see that this must have been a big issue because when His disciples got Him alone, they questioned Him about it. They wanted to know why Jesus answered the Pharisees' question with a question. Jesus had responded with another question because the Pharisees quoted only half of what the Law says about ending a marriage. They only asked if it was all right to put away (separate from) your wife. So Jesus forced them to admit that Moses commanded them to both *write a certificate of divorce* and *to put her away*. Jesus affirmed this correct answer by declaring that to only fulfill one of these requirements does not end a marriage in the eyes of God.

Separation Is Not Divorce

In the original Hebrew text, the word translated *divorce,* as in *the certificate of divorce,* was the word *keriythuwth,* or *kriytut,* meaning "a cutting (of the matrimonial bond) as in a divorce." *Sends her out of his house,* as it literally says in Deuteronomy 24:1, was derived from the Hebrew word *shalach* or *wshilachaah,* meaning, "to send away, for, or out." By examining the meaning of the words found in the original text, you can see that *divorce* referred to the cutting off, the denouncement or the doing away with of the matrimonial bond while the term *sends her out of his house* (put away) referred to the actual, physical carrying out of the divorce decree — the complete physical parting of a once-married couple. So divorce and separation are two different transactions that together constitute the legal and spiritual end of a marriage.

If your spouse says he or she is no longer happy with you and gives you a certificate of divorce, then leave. You are free to become another person's spouse. But to enter another marriage without first having a certificate of divorce and a permanent separation is committing adultery. Merely separating from your spouse does not constitute a legal end to your marriage. Your marriage is not automatically over just because there now is some distance between the two of you and you are no longer engaging in intimate, physical fulfillment. You must put forth the *certificate of divorce* and *put away* your spouse before you can go out and date and eventually get married to another person. Once you have ended your marriage with a divorce — a certificate of divorce and separation from your former spouse on a permanent, physical basis — you are free to marry someone else.

May a Woman Divorce Her Husband?

Since Deuteronomy 24 talks about the rules for a man divorcing his wife, this may raise the question of whether a woman had a right to serve her husband with a certificate of divorce. The Law in this case does not give any examples of a woman serving her husband with a divorce decree, and there is no mention of this being permissible. But, by considering the customs of that time, it becomes obvious why this was so. The Law was written during a period when women did not occupy places of authority in their communities. They were not privy to hearing the teaching of the Law, as were their male counterparts. So they would not have known that this right was available to them.

But Jesus later made it customary for all Believers to consider themselves equal in the sight of God, for His Word says in Galatians 3:28:

> **There is neither Jew nor Greek, there is neither slave nor free, there is neither male nor female; for you are all one in Christ Jesus.**

From the very beginning of the Church, women began to read the Scriptures and even play a part in spreading the Gospel. In fact, the very first person to carry the message of the Gospel — that Jesus had risen from the dead — was Mary Magdalene (John 20:17-18). So, thanks to Jesus, today a woman divorcing her husband is just as appropriate as a man divorcing his wife.

72

In 2 Corinthians 3:6, the Scripture says that the Spirit of the Law was to bring forth liberty and blessings, while the letter of the Law kills. As Christians, we are to conduct ourselves according to the Spirit of the Law. Therefore, women no longer must wait for their husbands to serve them with a divorce decree in order to bring peace in their home.

Let Your Nay Be Nay

You do not give your spouse divorce papers, separate from him or her, and then later come back together in a physically intimate way. If you do, you are fornicating. It does not matter how it feels, you are in sin. You cannot remain intimate once you have ended your marriage and have this be right with God anymore than you can separate from your spouse and pursue other potential mates. You cannot have it both ways. You can only be committed to one spouse at a time, and this commitment must consist of a marriage vow.

You might say, "Well, God understands." Yes, God understands that you are acting in disobedience, that you are placing your own physical feelings and personal opinion above His decreed Word. God said to put your ex-wife or ex-husband away; you should not jump back into bed with your former spouse, as if you were still married. God does not condone this. You are hindering the blessings of God in your life if you do. Once you put that piece of paper in your spouse's hand and let him or her go away from you, that person is no longer your spouse. Therefore, you must stay apart and not be physically intimate. If you want to have the need for sexual fulfillment satisfied, then you must remarry. This is what God has to say about it — like it or not.

IS DIVORCE A SIN?

Of course, there are people who do go back and forth with their ex-husbands or ex-wives. But the Bible explicitly states in Deuteronomy 24:4 that a former spouse cannot take his or her spouse again. To do so is to curse yourself and your inheritance. Yet, I have heard some Christian women say, "I'm waiting for my ex-husband." Well, what is he doing? "He's married to someone else. I'm waiting for him to finish with her so he will come back to me. He always does." If your ex-husband were to just come back to you, Deuteronomy 24:4 says this would be an abomination in the eyes of God. Stop waiting. Start your life afresh in the Lord. To give you any other advice is error.

Jesus is so serious about keeping His people from adultery and fornication that in Matthew 5:27-28, Jesus specifically instructs His disciples on how to avoid adultery:

> **"You have heard that it was said to those of old, 'You shall not commit adultery.'**
> **But I say to you that whoever looks at a woman to lust for her has already committed adultery with her in his heart."**

Jesus first reminds His disciples of the Law. Then He goes on to say that if a man looks upon a woman to lust after her, it is a done deal. Now, Jesus is *not* saying that if a man looks upon a woman with lust it counts as if he actually has already committed adultery with her, but that it is only a matter of opportunity and time. Why? Because a man will plot and maneuver things just to secure what he has already pictured in his mind.

However, if you ever find yourself looking, do not be fooled into thinking, "Well, I'm already guilty of adultery in

74

a spiritual sense because I looked with lust, so I might as well actually do it." No, just stop looking. Jesus is warning His disciples to watch how they look at women because if they look long enough to begin to lust, it will surely lead them to an occasion to do what is immoral.

Despite what anyone or any institution may claim, God has graciously given us the divorce decree. You are free to have a happy family life and be blessed as long as your marriage was properly ended in the eyes of God. This means there is no need for you to turn to fornication or adultery to fulfill your physical urges should your marriage go awry. You can still have this very real need met without violating the will of God, because the Lord says you may remarry.

Many Christians fail to see the reality of fornication and adultery as sin. They mistakenly think that just because their marriage is not working out as they want, it is all right to become involved in fornication and adultery. You are deceived if you think divorce is not right in the sight of God, yet it is okay to commit adultery. Not getting a divorce does not justify your being physically intimate with others outside of marriage.

Just take a look at the story of Abraham, his wife Sarah, and Abimelech in Genesis 20. Abraham said Sarah was his sister, and so Abimelech, the king of Gerar, sent and took Sarah to be his wife. Genesis 20:3 says:

> **But God came to Abimelech in a dream by night, and said to him, "Indeed you are a dead man because of the woman whom you have taken, for she is a man's wife."**
>
> **But Abimelech had not come near her; and he said, "Lord, will You slay a righteous nation also?**

"Did he not say to me, 'She is my sister?' And she, even she herself said, 'He is my brother.' In the integrity of my heart and innocence of my hands I have done this."

And God said to him in a dream, "Yes, I know that you did this in the integrity of your heart. For I also withheld you from sinning against Me; therefore I did not let you touch her.

"Now therefore, restore the man's wife; for he is a prophet, and he will pray for you and you shall live. But if you do not restore her, know that you shall surely die, you and all who are yours."

In the ninth verse, Abimelech says to Abraham:

"What have you done to us? How have I offended you, that you have brought on me and on my kingdom a great sin? You have done deeds to me that ought not to be done."

If you really care about the person you may be seeing, then you will stop being physically intimate after reading this.

This demonstrates just how serious adultery is in the eyes of God. God is concerned about the sanctity of the marriage covenant. There is no way you can read this account and think that God is in any way, shape, or form approving of adultery. Adultery is sin, no matter what the situation or reasoning. And just as Abraham's not trusting the Lord could have caused Abimelech to sin against God, being physically intimate with someone new before properly ending your previous marriage drags that person into your sin and the consequences of it.

Beware the Traditions of Men

Some Christians have told me, "My pastor says I am to remain with my spouse. He teaches that divorce is just about the worst thing there ever was." But then they sheepishly ask me, "So I cannot get a divorce, can I?" And I ask them, "Did God intend for you to stay in an abusive relationship?" No. Jesus did not die so you could be battered and abused.

Look at Matthew 19:8; Jesus confirms what I am telling you. Jesus says divorce was permitted because of the hardness of man's heart. In doing so, Jesus affirmed that God knows that there are people who are simply hardhearted and unwilling to walk in the truth. In order to free those wanting to do right but who are bound by those in disobedience through marriage (Genesis 2:24), God permitted divorce. So the certificate of divorce and the putting away of a spouse was designed and initiated by God, not the government.

"But, pastor, I was taught that the only reason I can get a divorce is if adultery is involved." When you stand before God, you are going to have to answer for what His Word says, not what tradition, your religion, or public opinion says (2 Corinthians 5:10). Not even your own thinking will cut it. God is going to judge you according to His Word. I highly recommend you stop going by what you have heard that Jesus said and start searching the Scripture for yourself.

"But my pastor showed me where Jesus said this in the Bible." Then allow me to add to what I have already shared with you regarding Jesus' teaching in Matthew 19:9, as translated in the King James Bible:

77

"And I say to you, whosoever shall put away his wife, except it be for fornication, and shall marry another, committeth adultery: and whoso marrieth her which is put away doth commit adultery."

In the time of Jesus, sexual immorality, such as fornication, was punishable by stoning to death (Leviticus 20:10, John 8:5). Therefore, in such instances, the certificate of divorce and the putting away that is normally required for a marriage to be legally ended in the eyes of God would obviously not have been needed. If your spouse committed fornication, you automatically qualified for an immediate, permanent separation by their stoning. So, Jesus was not adding to or changing the law, only recognizing the sum of the Law (Deuteronomy 24:1-4, Leviticus 20:10), as it pertains to marital relationships.

Again, divorce is not God's best but sometimes, because of man's free will, there is no other choice. Mark 3:5 shows that even Jesus Himself was grieved at times by the hardness of the hearts of people. If you are staying married to a disobedient person because you have been taught by religion that you cannot get a divorce, then you have allowed the traditions of men to make the Word of God of no effect in your life (Matthew 15:6). So, how can you hope for God's best?

Let God Bring You the Right Spouse

Once you have fulfilled the two requirements for ending your marriage, the Word of God says you can become another person's mate. But, this time do not make the same mistakes you made the last time. Do not sacrifice your commitment to God and accept something less than the best. You are too valuable and precious. The heavenly Father sent His Son to die for you, so you must be very special, regardless of what your previous spouse may have said or how you may be feeling.

If you wait on the Lord and seek Him, God will bring you the right spouse. But, you are going to have to be astute enough in the Word of God to know the difference between a gift from God and an impostor from Satan. Be sure to check out the biblical checklist below. This will help you discern your "fit" from any "counterfeit."

Psalms 112:

> **Praise the LORD! Blessed is the man who fears [reverences] the LORD, Who delights greatly in His commandments.**
>
> **His descendants will be mighty on earth; The generation of the upright will be blessed.**
>
> **Wealth and riches will be in his house, And his righteousness endures forever.**
>
> **Unto the upright there arises light in the darkness; He is gracious, and full of compassion, and righteous.**
>
> **A good man deals graciously and lends; He will guide his affairs with discretion.**
>
> **Surely he will never be shaken; The righteous will be in everlasting remembrance.**
>
> **He will not be afraid of evil tidings; His heart is steadfast, trusting in the LORD.**

His heart is established; He will not be afraid, Until he sees his desire upon his enemies.

He has dispersed abroad, He has given to the poor; His righteousness endures forever; His horn will be exalted with honor.

The wicked will see it and be grieved; He will gnash his teeth and melt away; The desire of the wicked shall perish.

Proverbs 31:10-31:

Who can find a virtuous [capable] wife? For her worth is far above rubies.

The heart of her husband safely trusts her; So he will have no lack of gain.

She does him good and not evil All the days of her life.

She seeks wool and flax, And willingly works with her hands.

She is like the merchant ships, She brings her food from afar.

She also rises while it is yet night, And provides food for her household, And a portion for her maidservants.

She considers a field and buys it; From her profits she plants a vineyard.

She girds herself with strength, And strengthens her arms.

She perceives that her merchandise is good, And her lamp does not go out by night.

She stretches out her hands to the distaff, And her hand holds the spindle.

She extends her hand to the poor, Yes, she reaches out her hands to the needy.

She is not afraid of snow for her household, For all her household is clothed with scarlet.

She makes tapestry for herself; Her clothing is fine linen and purple.

Her husband is known in the gates, When he sits among the elders of the land.

She makes linen garments and sells them, And supplies sashes for the merchants.

Strength and honor are her clothing; She shall rejoice in time to come.

She opens her mouth with wisdom, And on her tongue is the law of kindness.

She watches over the ways of her household, And does not eat the bread of idleness.

Her children rise up and call her blessed; Her husband also, and he praises her:

"Many daughters have done well, But you excel them all."

Charm is deceitful and beauty is passing, But a woman who fears the LORD, she shall be praised.

Give her of the fruit of her hands, And let her own works praise her in the gates.

1 Corinthians 11:1-3:

Imitate me, just as I also imitate Christ.

Now I praise you, brethren, that you remember me in all things and keep the traditions just as I delivered them to you.

IS DIVORCE A SIN?

But I want you to know that the head of every man is Christ, the head of woman is man, and the head of Christ is God.

1 Corinthians 6:14-18:

And God both raised up the Lord and will also raise us up by His power.

Do you not know that your bodies are members of Christ?

Shall I then take the members of Christ and make them members of a harlot? Certainly not!

Or do you not know that he who is joined to a harlot is one Body with her? For "the two," He says, "shall become one flesh."

But he who is joined to the Lord is one spirit with Him.

Flee sexual immorality. Every sin that a man does is outside the body, but he who commits sexual immorality sins against his own body.

Unfortunately, far too many people have abandoned God's Word when selecting a mate. This is comparable to an airline pilot taking off on a flight without first going through the safety checklist. If there is a plane crash, lives are needlessly lost all because of the pilot's negligence. Be sure you use the Word of God to evaluate your potential mate before making any commitment.

And finally, the best way to keep from getting a divorce is to always take time to be with your spouse. This is why the Lord God instructed the children of Israel not to go to war during the first year of their marriage. God wanted them to have a year's time to get their marriage on a solid foundation (Deuteronomy 24:5). Despite having made provisions for divorce as we know it, God is serious about married couples staying together.

How Should I Proceed With a Divorce?

Although it is meant to be redemptive, oftentimes a divorce can initially do more to invoke a fierce war than to bring about peace and the ultimate reconciliation that God intends. So, you need to be ready. You need to be prepared, and you need to weigh all things and take your time to make this very significant decision. It is times like these that you need to be, as Jesus said in Matthew 10:16, as wise as a serpent and as harmless as a dove. If divorce is the best way to put an end to what is robbing you and your family of peace, you need to be operating in the wisdom of God.

Part of God's wisdom relating to getting a divorce is found in Luke 14:28-30:

> **"For which of you, intending to build a tower, does not sit down first and count the cost, whether he has enough to finish it —**
> **"lest, after he has laid the foundation, and is not able to finish, all who see it begin to mock him,**
> **"Saying, 'This man began to build and was not able to finish.'"**

The Word of God warns that when a man endeavors to accomplish anything of importance without first examining the cost, he runs the risk of failure and disgrace. You do not want to enter into a divorce proceeding without first making sure you are fully prepared to handle all the ramifications. You need to first prepare for what your spouse may have in mind. Otherwise, you may very well lose more than you anticipated. And if you are not in a position to handle all the ramifications of divorcing your spouse, then seek a peaceful resolution — at least until you are in position.

Luke 14:31-32 goes on to add:

> **"Or what king, going to make war against another king, does not sit down first and consider whether he is able with tenthousand to meet him who comes against him with twenty thousand?**
> **"Or else while the other is still a great way off, he sends a delegation and asks conditions of peace."'**

Consider all the ramifications. How is a divorce going to affect you financially? How will it affect your children? What about all your possessions? How will you handle your spouse's potential response? Thinking your divorce through, weighing the answers to all these questions will help keep you from getting into a place of danger – physically or financially.

If your spouse has a history of violence, you will want to consider your safety and the safety of your children. Some angry partners have only one thing in mind: To annihilate their spouse and everything that has to do with them, including their children. Proverbs says that the wicked seek the blood of the righteous. This is why you must consider what the intent of your spouse will be so that you can safeguard yourself in advance. If your spouse is likely to be vindictive, then you need to keep this in the forefront of your mind so that you are prepared to handle this problem safely and intelligently.

You need to use every legal tool available. This includes discreetly consulting with police, lawyers, marriage counselors, pastors, family members, relatives, etc. Proverbs 11:14 says that there is safety in a multitude of counsel. You also need to protect yourself by documenting all threats and any legitimate reasons why a divorce is necessary. The Bible says in 2 Corinthians 13:1 that out of the mouth of two or three witnesses let every word be established. This word *established* means "to be made solid," so you need to make sure that all of your evidence will hold up in a court of law.

If you are not employed or have no means of caring for yourself, then you need to start making plans to acquire any money that you can. If you have children, you must be prepared to provide for them as a single parent. First Timothy 5 and Proverbs 31 speak of women who operate businesses out of their home. This may be an ideal example for a single parent to follow, in that he or she can then have the security of knowing that the children are being looked after. If this is not possible, do not feel guilty. While you may have to work outside of your home and will not be there all the time — and even may not able to give them everything you would like — at least your children are able to live in peace. You are now providing for them something money cannot buy.

If you do begin working outside of your home, do not lie to your employer about your responsibility to your children. Most employers are sympathetic and are used to having employees that are single parents. You have God's assurance in Proverbs 23:10-11 that He will see to it that you have the favor you need with your employer because He commanded it in His Word:

> **Do not remove the ancient landmark, Nor enter the fields of the fatherless;**
> **For their Redeemer is mighty; He will plead their cause against you.**

So you can see from the Scripture that God protects the single mothers and fatherless children.

Do not lie to your children about what is going on, because they know the truth. If they should ask you about their Dad or Mom, do not try to build up his or her character when he or she has very little. Do not bad-mouth your spouse either. Speak as much of the truth that your children can handle. Do not let your children think that God's Word doesn't work when your spouse's disobedience is what has caused your marriage to fail.

And finally, look forward to a brighter future for you and your children, because now you can all enjoy the peace of God. Forget the things that are behind you. Forget guilt or depression because your disobedient spouse turned on you and the family. Understand that people will refuse to forgive; people will even reject God, who is the ultimate giver of all good things, so how much more will they reject you when they discover that you are truly living for the Lord? Just keep thinking the best of everyone while looking out for you and your family.

FIVE

THE FOURTH CHOICE: RECONCILIATION

God is the one who instituted the covenant of marriage, but He is not the one who determines who you marry. You cannot blame God for the troubles you have in your marriage. Also, regardless of the challenges you may face, God's intent for this covenant relationship was that it would be a lifelong commitment filled with love, joy, intimacy, and fulfillment. God meant the man to cleave to his wife and for the two of them to be one flesh; separation and divorce were never in His plan. So, since *reconciliation* means, "to be joined back together after you have been apart," God is obviously in favor of it.

The institution of marriage is God's creation, not man's invention. But because not everyone is really committed to making their marriage work, it may or may not be advantageous for you to seek reconciliation with your spouse.

Say you have made mistakes and have not always honored your marriage covenant the way you should. Now you have finally come to terms with your past, have forgiven yourself, and are truly wanting to make things right between you and your mate. But your spouse is not willing to forget the past. Reconciliation on one side would make for an unhealthy relationship that would keep both parties frustrated, so that they are not able to grow in the things of the Lord. You do not ever want to be tied to a relationship that hinders you in your pursuit of the goodness of the Lord. As unfortunate as it is, in situations like this, one may have to put a spouse behind them.

Part of making your marriage work is doing as Paul says in Philippians 3:13-14:

> **Brethren, I do not count myself to have apprehended; but one thing I do, forgetting those things which are behind and reaching forward to those things which are ahead, I press toward the goal for the prize of the upward call of God in Christ Jesus.**

This press is work; it is going to take some effort. And if your spouse is not willing to make this effort, there is no point in trying to reconcile your marriage. Amos 3:3 poses the question "How can two walk together unless they agree?"

Reconciliation requires the effort of both parties. You must be willing to come together and agree. This will require a 100% commitment – not 50-50, or "I'll give as much as I get." You must both be willing to give unconditionally to each other.

Not everyone will purpose to do right – or to even do what is best. So, as hard as it may be, you cannot take it personally if your spouse is not willing to put forth the effort to make your marriage all that it could be. This is not necessarily a reflection on you. Moses had to tell the children of Israel to choose life in Deuteronomy 30:15-20. Such a choice would seem to be obvious. Still, many chose not to follow the way of life. There will always be those who will choose death, and the Bible says in 1 Corinthians 5:1-5 that you are to let such persons reap the results of their decision. Even in the Book of Hosea, the Lord God told the children of Israel to leave Ephraim alone when he had turned his back on God and lusted after idols (Hosea 4:17).

"Pastor, should I pray for my spouse's return without first requiring a change of heart?"

Absolutely not. You will only end up where you started. In fact, if you want your marriage to be all that God says it can be, you should not consider reconciling with your spouse unless he or she is willing to acknowledge God's Word as the standard for defining the roles of the husband and wife within your marriage. Remember that the Bible admonishes us to submit to one another in the reverence of God (Ephesians 5:21), as He gives us instruction in His Word. This will never happen unless your spouse accepts the principles found in the Word of God.

"Well, Pastor, how should I believe for my spouse's return?"

You should pray that laborers be sent across your spouse's path, according to Matthew 9:37-38. Hebrews 7:25 lets you know that Jesus is able to save to the uttermost. In other words, He is not only able to save your spouse, but

He is also able to save your marriage. So, your mate's redemption should be a part of your prayer. You should also pray that the eyes of his or her understanding would be enlightened (opened), as Paul says in Ephesians 2:18. Of course, you will also want to pray for your partner's specific needs, as well as for your own personal growth through this challenging time. The principle for praying for the needs of both you and your spouse can be found in Mark 11:24-26. Don't forget that in the twenty-sixth verse, you are commanded to forgive. In fact, throughout the Bible we are told that we are to forgive. Being able to forgive is the first step to true reconciliation.

Make Love Your Motive

Before you were married, even before you were born, the Lord God reconciled you to Himself. John 3:16 says the motive for this reconciliation was none other than love. Likewise, your motivation for seeking reconciliation should be love.

As a disciple of the Lord Jesus Christ, you are called to love *first*. You are called to follow His example and love your spouse despite all the challenges and differences that have troubled your marriage. You are to walk in love toward your husband or wife, even if he or she does not act or feel love towards you. You are called to make the first move to pursue whatever option is necessary to bring peace between you.

Contrary to popular opinion, love is not a feeling; love is an action. It is an act of your will. It has nothing at all to do with how you feel and everything to do with doing what is right. If you find yourself doubting whether you married the right person just because all of a sudden you don't feel like you are in love, then you are operating in confusion. You are headed for a lot of heartache if you don't quickly submit yourself to the Word of God.

Of course, this does not mean that you give your spouse license to abuse or take advantage of you. It simply means that you do not hold any anger or ill feelings toward your spouse and that you seek peace. Be as wise as a serpent and as harmless as a dove (Matthew 10:16). Seek the Holy Spirit's guidance and direction so you can fulfill your calling to be a minister of reconciliation (2 Corinthians 5:18). Desire that your spouse be reconciled to God and that, if it is not wise for you to remain together, your marital challenges will be resolved in peace. Do not ever lose sight of God's promise that as long as you walk in love and the wisdom of God, there's an abundant life in Christ Jesus awaiting you. You can expect peace and prosperity to overtake you when you are diligent to observe and do all that the Lord has commanded.

Remember, reconciliation is the joining back together of that which was broken apart. The Bible speaks of man needing to be reconciled to God because man originally enjoyed fellowship with God but broke off fellowship through disobedience. But thank God for His goodness and mercy that endures forever. Despite the failure of our forefather, Adam, the heavenly Father still desires to commune with each of us, just as Adam once did. After all, fellowship is why He created man (John 4:23).

So the Lord desires that all of humanity would be reconciled to Him. His Word says it is His desire that no man would perish but that all would come to everlasting life (1

IS DIVORCE A SIN?

Timothy 2:4). And so He has graciously made a provision
or way for us to be joined back together with Him.

John 3:16 says:

**But God so loved the world that He gave His
only begotten Son.**

In other words, God reconciled the world to Himself
by sending Jesus, His Son, to be our salvation. The heavenly Father did this out of His love for us — a love that is
true in that God freely gave His best. Therefore, He is not
going to force you or anyone else to accept this free gift.
You decide for yourself if you are going to accept God's
means of reconciliation — His display of love for you.

Now, you may say that you do not believe this and
think that you do not need to receive Jesus as your personal Lord and Savior. You may say, "Jesus was good
for momma and grandma, but He is not good for me."
You may say, "I'm going to do things my way; I'll take
my chances." So God, out of His infinite mercy, has called
me — and others like me — to tell you that you really
are not taking any chances by refusing to accept Jesus
Christ as your personal Lord and Savior. You are actually sealing your eternal future.

So I will be blunt: If you have not accepted Jesus, when
the time comes for you to face your eternal future, do not
say, "But I have not done anything to deserve this!" By
refusing Jesus, you will have a free ticket to hell. Direct and
nonstop. This may sound like a harsh and cruel thing to say,
but what would be even more harsh and cruel would be to
not be honest and up-front with you and let you just suffer
the consequences. See, it is not about what you have done

92

per se, but about what Adam, your predecessor, did on your behalf by his disobedience.

In 2 Corinthians 5:19, the Bible says

Now all things are of God, who has reconciled us to Himself through Jesus Christ, and has given us the ministry of reconciliation.

That is, that God was in Christ reconciling the world to Himself, not imputing their trespasses to them, and has committed to us the word of reconciliation.

Now then, we are ambassadors for Christ, as though God were pleading through us: we implore you on Christ's behalf, be reconciled to God.

God so loved the world that He reconciled the world to Himself. Through Jesus, His Son, the heavenly Father has done His part.

Now it is up to you; it's your turn. You must be willing to do your part. God is not going to do anything to force you. However, the Bible does say that every knee will bow and every tongue will confess that Jesus is Lord to the glory of God the Father (Philippians 2:9-10). In other words, eventually you will confess the truth that Jesus is Lord. The question — your option — is when are you going to make this confession? You can either do it now and accept reconciliation to God, or you can do it later — on your way to hell.

Reconciled to What?

Whether you choose to reconcile the troubles in your marriage through divorce or by coming to a resolution of your challenges, the question remains "Reconciled to what?" Well, in a marriage, God joins two distinct individuals into one. Therefore, every marriage is a unique entity on the earth and each marriage reflects its own uniqueness. To see the perfect image of God's original plan for bringing a man and a woman together in marriage, you have to look back to the very beginning. According to the Book of Genesis, Adam and Eve had the very first marriage that God instituted. Initially, they lived God's ideal for a married couple.

Adam and Eve both knew innocence and peace with God. Genesis 3:8 says that they heard the sound of the Lord God walking in the garden in the cool of the day. And, in Genesis 3:9, when the Lord God called to Adam, the Bible records Adam's response. So Adam and Eve obviously knew the presence of the Lord and were able to hear and distinguish His voice. This tells you that in the ideal marriage, both partners are very much aware of the presence of the Lord and can hear and distinguish His voice. This must mean that in an ideal marriage, both partners have a personal relationship with the Lord.

Throughout the very first chapters of the Book of Genesis, you can also see that Adam and Eve both had separate and distinct responsibilities to fulfill within their marital relationship. Since God had made Adam in His own image (Genesis 2:27), Adam's biggest responsibility was to be a reflection of God on the earth. Adam was to keep underfoot all things that were made by God. He was to exercise authority over everything that flew in the air, everything that crept upon the earth, and everything that swam in the water. Adam was, as it were, the lord over it all. And since Genesis

2:18 says God made the woman as a helper comparable to Adam, or as a help meet as some translations read, so then Eve's main responsibility was to help God's man fulfill God's will on the earth and to enjoy her ability to bring intimacy into his life. Together, they would enjoy this gift and look forward to giving the world children who would perpetuate God's plan in the earth. Ecclesiastes 9:9 says that intimacy is God's gift to man.

The ideal marriage can only be realized when the man and his wife seek their own responsibilities to God and to one another. God never intended for a woman to take the place of a man, or vice versa. The woman was taken out of the man and births man, but she is not equipped to be a man. This is why Peter warned the Church that they would do better to consider their wives as the weaker vessel. Peter was not saying that women are weak, but that their strengths were different. Women simply were not made to work in the same fashion as a man because their purpose was different from that of a man. For man was made to till the ground (Genesis 2:5), while woman was made so the man would not be alone (Genesis 2:18).

Just as a man was made to till the ground, so is he to cultivate his wife. By this, I mean that a husband is supposed to sow seeds of love, affection, appreciation, respect, care, provision, godly leadership, and protection in his wife. While he is a farmer, he is also like a type of seed. His wife, on the other hand, is like fertile soil. She will eventually multiply whatever he puts into her. Women possess the innate ability to bring increase. This is why husbands should want their wives' input in everything they do. Men must also realize that it is for this very reason that whatever they give their wives will come back to them multiplied. This is why the Bible says in Ephesians 5:28 that he who loves his wife loves himself. So, if a man gives his wife a little grief, she will naturally repay him with more grief. If he gives his wife some attention, she will give him love, admiration, and great physical intimacy. And because men innately initiate things, while women typically respond to things, there are a lot of men who are catching hell from the seeds sown in their mates by other men. There are a lot of unhappy women who, years later, are still reacting to something some man did or failed to do.

In the perfect marital relationship, the man walks in the image of God and the woman walks in submission to her husband, as to the Lord. The husband is supposed to be as Christ in the home. He is supposed to give up his desires, lay down his life, and walk in the life that God would provide for him. He is supposed to be like a type of Christ. Therefore, he is to love his wife just as Jesus loves the Church. His wife, on the other hand, is supposed to respect and support her husband as his help meet (able helper) while also fulfilling their need for physical intimacy. Her rightful position is by her husband's side.

This is born out in Ephesians 5:21-33:

> **Submitting to one another in the fear of God** [as God has instructed you].
>
> **Wives, submit to your own husbands, as to the Lord.**
>
> **For the husband is the head of the wife, as also Christ is head of the church; and He is the Savior of the body.**

Therefore, just as the church is subject to Christ, so let the wives be to their own husbands in everything.

Husbands, love your wives, just as Christ also loved the church and gave Himself for her,

That He might sanctify and cleanse her with the washing of water by the word,

That He might present her to Himself a glorious church, not having spot or wrinkle or any such thing, but that she should be holy and without blemish.

So husbands ought to love their own wives as their own bodies; he who loves his wife loves himself.

For no one ever hated his own flesh, but nourishes and cherished it, just as the Lord does the church.

For we are members of His body, of His flesh and of His bones.

"For this reason a man shall leave his father and mother and be joined to his wife, and the two shall become one flesh."

This is a great mystery, but I speak concerning Christ and the church.

Nevertheless let each one of you in particular so love his own wife as himself, and let the wife see that she respects her husband.

The wife's love for her husband is understood by him through her respect and submission to his godly leadership. The husband's love for his wife is understood by her through his provision for her and their family, as well as his willingness to love her unconditionally, just as Jesus gave up His life. Jesus' giving was exemplified both by His lifestyle of love that He gave daily (1 Peter 2:21) and ultimately in His willingness to die on the cross.

If you want to see how your marriage should function, look at how Jesus Christ relates to the Church. After all, the Church is referred to as the Bride of Christ (Revelation 21:2; 22:17). Through the Gospels, you can see that Jesus has concern for His Bride, the body of Christ. He is willing to take upon Himself the responsibility of providing for her in every way. He leads her by precept and example, word and deed. He received His instruction for her from His Father God. He has spent time washing His Bride with the water of the Word. And His aim has always been to present to Himself a glorious Church absent from blemishes and imperfections in character and appearance. Jesus expects the husbands to follow His example and consult Him when they do not understand. He has provided His local churches to help bring man to the point where he can receive from Him.

As we saw in Genesis, chapter 20, Abraham lied by not telling the servants of King Abimelech, the king of Gerar, that Sarah was his wife, even though she was in fact his sister. Therefore, Abimelech, desiring such a fine woman as Sarah, sent for and took her. But God intervened. In the third verse, God came to King Abimelech in a dream by night and said, "Behold, you are a dead man, for the woman you have taken is another man's wife." So we see right from the start of the Bible that God is very concerned about the marital relationships of His people, so seriously concerned that He visited Abimelech in a dream and threatened his life! You, too, should take the covenant of marriage seriously.

The Fourth Choice: Reconciliation

Because of the strong stand that I have taken, some may get the impression that I am in favor of separation and divorce as the only way to resolve the issues of a difficult marriage. This could not be further from the truth. My sole intent has been only to give insight and positive guidance to counteract improper views on separation, divorce, and the toleration of a dysfunctional marriage. I assure you that my desire is that all marriages would succeed and prosper, even as God desires all to be reconciled.

The Word of God is consistently clear about marriage being honorable in all (Hebrews 13:4). Although many attacks have come against marriage and the family, this God-given institution remains the firm foundation of society. Never forget that God intended it to be a means of thoroughly enjoying the abundant life that Christ Jesus came to give you. If you are facing trouble in your marriage, remember that in order to enjoy life as God meant it to be, you will have to do as my wife and I admonished you right from the start:: Step out in faith. You will have to take the steps necessary, based on God's Word, to bring a godly resolution to whatever is challenging the peace of your family environment. Once you take that first step in faith, the Lord will be with you every step of the way to direct and guide you as long as you continue to acknowledge Him.

For a complete list of books and tapes by
Pastor Frederick K.C. and Betty R. Price, please write

Pastor Fred and Betty Price
Crenshaw Christian Center
P.O. Box 90000
Los Angeles CA 90009

Or visit our WebSite at:

www.faithdome.org

BOOKS BY FAITH ONE PUBLISHING

BY BETTY R. PRICE
STANDING BY GOD'S MAN

THROUGH THE FIRE & THROUGH THE WATER
My Triumph Over Cancer

LIFESTYLES OF THE RICH & FAITHFUL

BY FREDERICK K.C. PRICE

HOW FAITH WORKS

IS HEALING FOR ALL?

HOW TO OBTAIN STRONG FAITH
Six Principles

NOW FAITH IS

THE HOLY SPIRIT --
The Missing Ingredient

FAITH, FOOLISHNESS, OR PRESUMPTION?

THANK GOD FOR EVERYTHING?

HOW TO BELIEVE GOD FOR A MATE

LIVING IN THE REALM OF THE SPIRIT

THE ORIGIN OF SATAN

CONCERNING THOSE WHO HAVE FALLEN ASLEEP

HOMOSEXUALITY:
State of Birth or State of Mind?

WALKING IN GOD'S WORD
Through His Promises

PRACTICAL SUGGESTIONS FOR SUCCESSFUL MINISTRY

NAME IT AND CLAIM IT!
The Power of Positive Confession

THE VICTORIOUS, OVERCOMING LIFE
(A Verse-by-Verse Study on the Book of Colossians)

A NEW LAW FOR A NEW PEOPLE

THE PROMISED LAND
(A New Era for the Body of Christ)

THREE KEYS TO POSITIVE CONFESSION

THE WAY, THE WALK,
AND THE WARFARE OF THE BELIEVER
(A Verse-by-Verse Study on the Book of Ephesians)

BEWARE! THE LIES OF SATAN

TESTING THE SPIRITS

IDENTIFIED WITH CHRIST:
A Complete Cycle From Defeat to Victory

THE CHRISTIAN FAMILY:
Practical Insight for Family Living
(formerly MARRIAGE AND THE FAMILY)

THE HOLY SPIRIT:
THE HELPER WE ALL NEED

FIVE LITTLE FOXES OF FAITH

BUILDING ON A FIRM FOUNDATION

DR. PRICE'S GOLDEN NUGGETS
A Treasury of Wisdom for Both Ministers and Laypeople

LIVING IN HOSTILE TERRITORY
A Survival Guide for the Overcoming Christian

THE TRUTH ABOUT ... BOOK SERIES